DISMAZED AND DRIVEN:
My Look at Family Homelessness in America

Charles Bruce Foundation, Carlisle, Pennsylvania

Cover Design: Chad Bruce, Charles Bruce Foundation Photos: Diane Nilan, HEAR US Inc.
Layout and Interior Design: Maxwell Donnelly

Printed in the United States of America.

Proceeds from this book will benefit HEAR US Inc. 115 E. Ogden Ave. #105-329, Naperville, IL 60563, a not-for-profit organization dedicated to giving voice and visibility to families and youth experiencing homelessness. More info, contact Diane@hearus.us

www.hearus.us

TABLE OF CONTENTS

DEDICATION

To Congressman John Lewis,
Your example leaves me with no excuse.
Your challenge to me, to cause "good trouble,"
leaves me with a roadmap.

To Christen,
Your life was not in vain.
Your encouragement of me
fuels my passion.

To Karen,
Your life of love and service
set a standard I could only hope to replicate.

ACKNOWLEDGEMENTS

Thanks...for the kids.

Let me assure you that if not for my love of kids, and those listed below who share that love, this book wouldn't exist. On behalf of the millions of kids experiencing homelessness, let me thank my friends who played a significant role in bringing Dismazed and Driven to reality:

ART, PUBLISHING

Pat LaMarche—Babe of Wrath, editor and encourager-in-chief
    for this book
Chad Bruce—artist, and force behind publishing

EDIT, ENCOURAGE, EVALUATE

Judy Gale Borich
Lani Anacan Breidenstein
Heather Denny
Max Donnelly
Richard Guzman
Barbara Wand James
Anita Levine
Darlene Newsom
Jeremy Rosen
Mark Saxenmeyer
Pat Van Doren
Yvonne Vissing
Joe Willard

GURUS

Barbara Duffield
Laura Vazquez

SCHOOL PARTNERS – sheroes and heroes

All who work to connect kids to school (McKinney-Vento liaisons),
    despite the challenges of homelessness, who trusted me to gather

stories of kids and families, who took time to help me when you had no time, who let me park, plug in, and shower.

SHELTER/ADVOCATE PARTNERS – more sheroes and heroes

My abysmal administrative skills fail me when it comes to pulling out the names of all the dedicated people who trusted me enough to connect me with families to interview, places to park, and so much more.

TECH SUPPORT– keeping me connected with the world

Ken Johnson – U.S. IT Systems
Daniel Riefstahl – Pixel Point Creative

TRAVEL SUPPORT – keeping my vehicles rolling

Kathy, Vicky, Jim and all at Bockman's Truck and Fleet

TRUSTED EXPERTS – kids and parents who know lots about homelessness

Those who trusted me to share their stories. They knew I meant it when I said I'd share their stories far and wide. Without you, my journey would have no meaning. With you, my life, especially the past 15 years, surpassed my wildest dreams for attaining a purpose. I hope I did justice to your stories.

WRITING SUPPORT – making sure I have a good place to park, meals, and all I needed to write

Benedictine Sisters of Lisle, HEAR US Inc. Board and Donors, Julia Jilek and Sharon Adee, Sass & Chuck Wanzer.

There comes a point where
we need to stop
just pulling people out of the river.
We need to go upstream and find out
why they're falling in.

- Desmond Tutu

INTRO

Big lesson: never say never. As in I'd never travel/camp, much less live, in a house on wheels.

I spent the bulk of my driving life scoffing at motorhomes that slogged along in front of me. In a bit of reverse-snobbery, my tent camping days—from Girl Scout adventures to paddling around in the Northwoods of Minnesota's Boundary Waters—emboldened my "that's not camping" attitude towards recreational vehicles, aka RVs. That was then, before 15 years of living in a small RV, on a mission to do what no one has done.

I've spent 15 years on America's backroads chronicling the plight and promise of families experiencing homelessness. I've seen what countless interstate highway travelers or those flying over at 40,000 feet don't see. I've witnessed the unheralded survival of courageous parents and kids whose homes have vanished for countless reasons. I've faced down and looked up to those with the power to change a system that seems to perpetuate homelessness. I've encountered America, good, bad and ugly, about 400,000 miles of it, in every state except Alaska. And I've done it living in a small motorhome.

What would motivate someone to choose this unconventional lifestyle? What principle merits discarding the norms of stability and moderate comfort? What greater good could make a person chase around in the boonies, far from family, friends and familiar territories?

This appropriately unconventional book, part memoir and part social narrative, will take you on my journey which started in 2005 with the founding of my unique nonprofit, HEAR US Inc. With the mission of "giving voice and visibility to families and youth experiencing homelessness," I began a sojourn that unfolded day by day. I wanted to hear from those most familiar with homelessness, those most invisible and those most misunderstood. I wanted to be the instrument to let their voices be heard and their faces be seen.

The primary reason I set out on this quirky odyssey way back in 2005? To raise awareness of children and youth experiencing homelessness so they could, at the very least, enjoy school stability. Homeless kids getting into school, as you will see, has been at the core of my existence for a good part of the past 30-plus years of my life. But it doesn't just stop at the schoolhouse door. No. I want them to be able to open the door of a place to call home.

Embracing this undertaking makes a difference in the lives of millions of kids and adults experiencing homelessness. Hopefully it will continue to shine a light on the myriad issues and injustices that create and compound family homelessness.

I'm constantly dismazed by how few people grasp the reality, the scope and suffering of homeless families. Yes, a small contingent of dedicated women and men work on the systemic side of this issue. Though they shine a light through media contacts and shape policies on the federal and state level, I still have people asking incredulously, "Families are homeless?"

My unorthodox approach raising awareness about family homelessness included naively thinking I could attract media attention to raise this issue like a flag on the Fourth of July. While I've managed to attract some media attention, it's far less than I hoped. I couldn't have known this would be the era when mainstream media would be attacked, gutted like a catfish, and cast to waiting seagulls. In the meantime, the faux news bile surges over various forms of social media, distracting, distorting and debilitating our gallant efforts.

Longtime friends who worked as respectable journalists for mainstream media have retired, been ousted, or have squeezed themselves into an alternate role that allows them to address social issues on other platforms. I get it. That's in essence what I did. One big difference: my journalist friends knew their trade. They had skills. Me, I had no idea of what I got into.

Fast forward to 2020...

HEAR US 2020 VisionQuest, my latest official project, took me all across Route 20 in the northern part of the country and along I-20 through a broad swath of the south. In many ways this journey was my vision quest. I reflected on my life. I pondered homelessness and how it far exceeded what I had imagined. I contemplated the importance of my one-woman nonprofit, HEAR US Inc. I recognized that my travels gifted me with the opportunity to listen and share stories that would otherwise go untold. Then I, and the world, hit a speedbump—Covid-19.

Bear with my quirky storytelling style. It unfurls like the lives of those stuck in a massive traffic jam. My stops-and-starts, the bits and pieces of stories from my life and travels mix in with the often agonizing and inspiring accounts from the families I met. It will upend some of you. Good. Those ensconced in stability need to experience what it's like to step into traffic, unprotected by a sturdy vehicle, and weave through the chaos of cars and trucks zipping by with no regard for your existence.

Having ample time to think as I ambled across the highways and byways, I've identified culprits and champions in this arena of family homelessness. I will illustrate the dismazing dangers of continuing on our nation's unenlightened route to address family homelessness. I will chart an alternate course to meet the needs of millions of upended families.

Rather than obsess over an orderly succession of events, I invite you to follow my theme—driving. It's appropriate for what my life has been these past 15 years. This narrative will take you where you never chose to go. The journey will hopefully change your thinking about a largely unchecked social issue. One that, if ignored, will lead to unabated homelessness for millions more families.

Disclaimers:

To be clear, I'm not homeless, though I don't have a permanent home. I have modest resources. This unconventional journey was by choice. I have gone to great lengths to not be a "poverty pimp" – a person using their position with people in poverty to get rich. Unlike the stereotypical preachers who fly around in private jets from their mansions to their estates, I've paid for the van, maintenance and expenses out of my pocket.

My representation of families experiencing homelessness does not depict all who find themselves in this situation. Many families experience horribly devastating conditions, living far worse than those in shelters, doubled up, in motels or in other locations. I did not pursue their stories for countless reasons. The stories I relate are, I believe, representative of a multitude of families in the "middle" where their housing is lost for a variety of reasons. Their lives are disrupted. Their well-being imperiled. Their options limited by poverty and reality. Their circumstances dire.

I chose to omit the subpopulation of unaccompanied homeless youth (UHY) in this book for several reasons. First, that topic deserves a book of its own, one I'd not be as qualified to write. While I encountered and interviewed several UHYs along my journey, I interviewed many more families. For the record, my own family members have spent time on the streets as youth, so it's not that I don't care about the issue.

Ditto about kids in foster care. Their tie to homelessness, especially for UHY, is sadly substantial. Foster care is a topic that needs to stand on its own, written by someone who grasps the intricacies of that beleaguered system.

My stories about families represent them as accurately as I could, given what I know. Most details were validated by those who connected me with my subjects, filtered by my street sense and common sense. Those families gave me permission to share their stories, and I promised to do that far and wide. I hope I did them justice. If I didn't, I am sorry beyond what I could convey.

I decided not to identify my subjects by race unless it was relevant. I can tell you that the stories contained in the book, and those I gathered on video, are diverse in race, geographic location, education levels, and along so many more demographics.

I opted to not include names of homeless liaisons and others secondary to my stories. You know who you are, and you know I hold you in deep esteem.

Memory being fickle, I've relied on my journals, photos, social media posts, news stories, and blogs to fill in the blanks of my recollections. I've tried not to sensationalize my accounts. Maybe I've understated, but my sister would tell you, I hate drama.

The references listed at the end are helpful sources of more information on this issue.

I'm bipartisan pissed. I've worked with capable, compassionate Republicans and clueless, callous Democrats. And vice versa.

I'm a lousy tourist, rarely taking time to stop at attractions that others have waited a lifetime to visit. This will not be a travel guide. Although, you might pick up some quirky features of places I've been.

I'll bounce around the 15 years of my travels, preferring to follow a thematic pattern instead of a timeline.

Other Things About Your Dismazed Driver

Answers to the questions I get all the time:

- I'm single, never married, no kids. Not looking to change that.
- I was going to be a nun, a Joliet Franciscan, but ended that journey back in 1973. I'm still on good terms with the Sisters who taught me from grade school through college, including a delightful group of women who shepherded me through high school. They continue to marvel at how their teachings worked on me.
- For fun, when I have the opportunity, I'll enjoy a solo game of disc golf, or kayak with a friend or alone. I'm pretty much a buzz-kill.
- I don't have a pet, though I have dog-pals along the way. I'd have a dog, but my lifestyle isn't conducive to responsible pet ownership. I'm allergic to cats.
- I really like my tiny lifestyle. You couldn't have told me that before I started.
- I'm not afraid staying by myself.
- I believe most people are good at heart, some a tad unenlightened.
- Every path I've traveled in my 30+ years working in homelessness has been unconventional. Even so, I could not have imagined what I've done since 2005.

- Yes, I have always loved to drive, but to think I'd spend 15 years on the road, living full-time in a small camper, traveling nearly 400,000 miles of mostly backroads while chronicling family and youth homelessness? Not in my wildest career plan!

You Need to Know

Not all RV camping is the same. A road-worn 32' Allegro camper parked in an evergreen Washington State campground looked like every other RV. Then the inhabitants poured out: two grandmothers, husband and wife, their two children, and 5 dogs. Before you let your mind go down the "what the hell?" track, let me add a few details that offer a perspective.

This is homelessness. Everyone in this camper lost their place to live. The grannies, owners of 4 of the dogs, were taken in by the parents of the two kids. One: a giant of an 11-year-old boy. The other: a quiet 4-year-old girl. And their dog. The family lost their place to live when their vehicle—a worn cargo van that dad could use to get to his two part-time jobs—became a financial millstone. The $200-a-week payment on an extortion-like loan broke them. The van was repossessed, but the payments will continue for eternity, or until their repossessed vehicle gets paid off. The family moved into a 20-year-old camper, and for months have been shuffling between places to park. Because of their credit problems, including the rip-off van loan, subsidized housing won't happen. Getting any housing is doubtful.

Questioning the financial decisions that contributed to the upheaval of three combined households is as pointless as questioning how auto dealers can sell to someone with inadequate income, charge them sky-high interest, and later repossess the vehicle to resell it in much the same manner.

The fact is, this is homelessness: the kind that our country has ignored for decades, the kind I've pursued for the past 15 years from the vantage point of my little camper/full-time home and my video camera.

Sometimes the people around you won't understand your journey. They don't need to, it's not for them.

- Joubert Botha

CHAPTER 1
Meet the Dismazed Driver

Of course, everything we do is connected, and as I look in the rearview mirror of my life, I can see how one path led to another. I invite you to hop into the passenger seat and travel with me. To do so, it will be helpful to know from where I came before I hit the road.

Beginning Daze

I stumbled into the world of social services—all spent in the field of homelessness— because of years-long unemployment in the early 80s when the bottom dropped out of the economy. I started working a contract job at Joliet (Illinois) Catholic Charities, spearheading the agency's preparation for accreditation. I had no idea what that entailed, but it was a job, and I was more than tired of standing in the unemployment line.

In the mid-80s homeless people poured into this small, limited services agency at a rate far beyond what had been "normal." My boss pointed to me, the one person with only one task, and said "You take on homelessness." My reply, "What do I know about homelessness? I'm not a social worker," did nothing to stop my initial journey down this path. Ironically, my tenuous hold on that 6-month job turned into an unplanned career because of homelessness.

I started an emergency shelter in Joliet in 1987 with little more than chutzpah and a lot of community support. I learned from shelter gurus in nearby counties. I had a lot to learn and fast. Lives depended on it—those who relied on our overnight winter shelter and the volunteers who bravely entered this new arena every night.

Silly me, the philosophy major—I wondered what was upstream. Why were so many people landing on the streets? Naively, I figured if we could stem the tide, we'd all be better off. One of my earliest mentors was Mitch Snyder, the much-heralded activist who pushed President Reagan into a corner, forcing the feds to get involved in homelessness. Mitch, with his unparalleled penchant for drawing the media into the issue, made me see that the only way to serve in this cause was to put an equal amount of effort into systemic advocacy.

Shelter Express Lane

In 1990, I began working at the largest emergency shelter in Illinois outside Chicago in Aurora, Hesed House, a former city incinerator converted into a center for ministry. I ran the shelter for 13 years. When I took that job, I had only three years' experience in homelessness. Not enough to prepare me for what came at me in that next phase. Besides recruiting, training and overseeing 5,000 volunteers who "staffed" our shelter, I needed to keep order in a naturally chaotic nighttime environment. Hesed House was "home" to 100 or more men, women and children.

Contrary to popular opinion on how to run shelters, Hesed House's model, Public Action to Deliver Shelter (PADS), was based on hospitality. It was our feeble attempt to soften the experience of homelessness by not running the shelter like a police state. It really did make a difference, resulting in a relatively peaceful atmosphere defying the expectations of the unknowing.

We opened our doors to anyone—single adults and families—who remained respectful in our cramped quarters. The biggest drawback? It was an emergency overnight shelter that – at the time – operated from October 1, to the middle of May. Because we relied on volunteers from faith communities to cover three shifts a night, the shelter founders felt year-round would be a lot to ask. Volunteers staffing the shelter, a monumental task, continues to this date, almost 40 years after this "emergency" response started.

Soon after I landed at Hesed House, I started our Tent City. According to Michael Stoops, a key staffer at the National Coalition for the Homeless, it was the first municipally-sanctioned operation of its kind. During our shelter's off-season, mid-May to October, we operated an unconventional campground that became home for about 60 men, women and eventually a handful of families.

When I first started this work, I feared what could happen at any given time in our shelter. Once I decided to let down my guard, I discovered that people staying in this overcrowded, inadequate facility were *gasp* people. The process of discovery— my humanity and theirs—offered a different, more satisfying— albeit challenging—experience. I still had to keep order. I was known as the "benevolent sheriff (or dictator)." But things ran smoothly considering the dreadful possibilities. The sense of solidarity—staff, volunteers and guests (as we respectfully called them)—contributed to a fairly consistent sense of order. When things got out of hand (for example, someone having a really bad night and going off in the middle of a crowded dining room) I could intervene without all hell breaking loose. And I always knew I had an unsanctioned, but earnest backup team ready to spring into action – the same guys who stayed in this sardine can.

Undoubtedly, the hardest part of my job was working with the families. My previous teaching years gave me classroom management experience. That, plus being the oldest of five kids, made me a tad rigid. Looking back, my expectations of parents, typically mothers, were often unreasonable. Horrible circumstances drove these families to our shelter. Then we crammed them into a small (15' x 15') space, with plastic-covered mats wedged in for sleeping. No dividers. No privacy. The family room filled to overcrowding: often 3-5 families with what seemed like 1,000 kids. We knew nothing about the impact of trauma on kids and adults. Our ignorance inadvertently compounded their trauma.

Over my 13 years there, many families drifted in and out. A handful stayed much longer, or returned multiple times. Those are etched in my memory. I'm still in contact with some, thanks to social media. I became privy to the complex causes of their homelessness—often situations laced with abuse, frequently sexual, always poverty. Too commonly the parents had experienced the same as kids. Dysfunctional? Yes, but also beautiful in so many ways.

Most of the kids went to school. I didn't pay much attention to this essential aspect of childhood at first. I didn't think about how they fit in. Whether they had their essential supplies. If they did their homework. If they'd had the money for their class field trip. On occasion I got jolted into awareness, "tomorrow is Halloween and my kid needs a costume." That meant a trip downstairs to our Clothes Closet and a heap of creativity.

I did try to settle them down to sleep at a decent hour, because they were officially awakened at 5:30 when they joined the morning hustle to get breakfast, a bagged lunch, clear out of the family room, and head off to school. It's a routine that repeats in countless programs nationwide today.

I vaguely recall incidents when the school required missing documents for enrollment, leaving the student sitting school-less in our shelter. This was before we pushed for passage of the Illinois Education for Homeless Children Act in 1994. Because I had shelter-running details distracting me—ordering blankets, scabies infestations, figuring out how to get money to pay for laundry soap—I never developed relationships with school personnel, relationships that would have been beneficial for the families. I just never thought of that as my job.

Turbocharged Force for Change

In addition to the grueling shelter work, our program professed a strong belief in systemic advocacy. My training under Mitch and others was put to good use. We recognized the tremendous resource we had—thousands of volunteers with first-hand contact to "the homeless." We nurtured these volunteers into citizen-advocates. They could contact their legislators as voters, demanding attention to these seemingly unimportant issues. We developed regular campaigns aimed at changes to unjust laws and policies—food stamp cuts, slashed human service budgets, etc. We led the charge in the state and nation for systemic advocacy. We experienced occasional success: Passage of the Illinois Homeless Voters' Rights Act; the Illinois Housing Trust Fund; and the Illinois Education for Homeless Children Act. We repelled draconian cuts to the nation's homeless budget. Most incredible of all, we helped pass the federal McKinney-Vento Education for Homeless Children Act (SchoolHouse Connection, 2020) in 2002.

By no means were we successful in every campaign. But we did develop a reputation as relentless advocates. Relentless fits me. Someone described me as a dog with a bone. Driven. I started sensing the way to work these systems—getting to know legislative staff in Springfield or Washington, honing relationships with journalists to further our cause, and developing creative campaigns to stand out from the tried-and-true protest marches.

I plunged into leadership of statewide homelessness and housing coalitions. I learned as I went. It was evident that this aspect of poverty and homelessness advocacy was far from a sophisticated movement. We tried. We won some and lost too many. David vs. Goliath is an apt comparison. Advocacy required more time and energy than what any of us had, but we were determined, hoping to reduce the downstream impact that resulted in more and more kids and adults in homeless situations.

The Long Road to Justice

Little did I recognize what was evolving in our most significant campaign: fighting for the rights of homeless kids to go to school. As this effort intensified, it became the driving force in my life.

The journey started out simply enough. When Tyeast Boatwright, a mother of three, staying in our transitional shelter, asked to see me in August 1993, I had no idea what was unfolding. Her family had been living in Naperville, an affluent community on the east edge of Aurora, doubled up with a friend following Tyeast's divorce. They lived there a couple years before the landlord caught on. They had to leave or their host family would also lose their housing. Kerplunk into our shelter.

In August, when Tyeast tried re-enrolling her kids in their schools, she was told, "No." She was instructed to enroll them in the district containing our shelter. That seemed wrong to her, thus the visit to my office. We examined the existing federal law, the McKinney Act, a nebulous statute that hinted at school stability with loopholes a semi-tractor trailer could drive through. She wanted what every mother wanted—the best for her kids. They had been doing well in their schools, and school stability was important.

She was willing to challenge the school district, and I promised the support of our rag-tag advocacy team. Fortunately, this was an issue that resonated with many reporters I knew—TV, radio and print—who got caught up in this human interest story. We staged visual demonstrations to call attention to this injustice, marching on the school district office with life-sized cardboard cutouts symbolizing the three school-less kids.

The school district evidently wanted to crush us like bugs on the windshield, suing the mom to put an end to this legal battle. Undaunted, we countersued, thanks to a social-justice minded lawyer willing to represent her pro bono. A two-month court battle ensued, and Tyeast lost on a technicality. But the loss propelled us into a new arena—we had to get a state law passed. The federal law merely allowed for the homeless student to finish the school year at their original school. We wanted to close the gap, allowing students to stay for the duration of their homelessness. Tyeast's kids had technically finished the year in their old schools.

We packed our hallmark state law, the Illinois Education for Homeless Children Act, with common sense requirements. We included school stability, good for the length of homelessness; immediate enrollment; transportation; and academic supports to help the student succeed. Our goal: removing barriers that commonly existed when students without a home tried to get an education.

We named the legislation, "Charlie's Bill," after an adorable boy in a photo taken by photojournalist Pat Van Doren. Four-year-old Charlie and his mom had stayed at our shelter, and the picture of him holding a stray cat, his belly hanging out, with untied shoes on the wrong feet, conveyed "every child." His mom agreed to let us use his iconic image for our campaign. I still use his image in my nonprofit's logo. And I'm still in contact with Charlie and his family.

Incredibly, we found bipartisan legislative support beyond what we could have dreamt. The bill passed the first time around, a rare happening for something involving homelessness. To our great surprise and delight it was signed into law, and went into effect September, 1994.

"Charlie's Law" quickly became the envy of other states. Instead of the labor-intensive process of state-by-state passage of a similar bill, we looked to the federal McKinney-Vento Act which was up for reauthorization. Congress had a chance to fix or nix the law. In 1998, newly-elected Republican Congresswoman Judy Biggert, from Illinois' 13th district, toured our facility. By then our unique "tent city" housed a few families. Judy was new to homelessness, and was shell-shocked at the end of the tour. She asked what she could do to help. I blurted out, "Get Charlie's Law passed on the national level!" Amazingly, she agreed to champion the cause. She knew us from our state campaign. She was a state representative then. Little did any of us know where this would take us, especially me.

Another Route Change

The story of "Charlie's Law" is best told in my book, *Crossing the Line: Taking Steps to End Homelessness*, a reader-friendly tome I wrote to remove the fear factor for potential shelter volunteers. I had time to write after my shelter job came to an unexpected end in 2003. Suffice to say, things happen in nonprofit management. I was on the losing side of a long-running conflict that found me stretched beyond capacity as I attempted to overcompensate for what I saw as inadequate leadership. The outcome was grueling. I loved what I did and couldn't imagine doing anything else. But good came from painful.

After the federal law, McKinney-Vento Education for Homeless Children and Youth Act, passed in 2002, and after my unexpected need for a career change arose, I applied to create and run a regional program. Project REACH helped schools implement the new McKinney-Vento law. My territory included 305 school districts in the 8 counties surrounding the City of Chicago. My staff of three full-time and one part-time passionate and knowledgeable women made our region rock. When it rocked too hard—fighting for a student wrongly denied their educational rights—I took over.

I'd sit in a room with highly-paid lawyers, school officials and the family. When all was said and done, we won every dispute. Little did I know that this would cause another unexpected change for me.

As I conducted professional development trainings with educators, it became apparent that a good number of school personnel and administrators had never come in contact with families experiencing homelessness. Their lack of awareness led to much confusion and unnecessary suffering. By the time our office got involved in disputes, the situation had gone too far. The student typically had missed school, the family was flabbergasted that their children's education was disrupted, and the school had ventured into legal peril.

Driven to Desperation

A colleague in DC, Barbara Duffield, and I agreed that a short professional development video featuring children talking about their homelessness and what school meant to them would be beneficial. The film would help educators understand homelessness from kids' viewpoints. We got a grant, hired a film crew, and prepared to start filming in early April 2005. The last week of March I was told that my highly-praised, effective project would be restructured by my supervisors who had no clue about this issue. Damn! Another unplanned career change.

I knew I needed to get creative for my next chapter. I knew I never wanted to work for someone else again. I didn't want to leave this issue behind, knowing that a film depicting kids talking about their homeless and school would be an indispensable tool. I made an audacious decision.

I'd make the film.

I sold my townhouse, car and most of my possessions, bought a small motorhome (self-funded), started a nonprofit organization, HEAR US Inc. I raised enough money to get started, purchased a professional-grade video camera and equipment with grant funds, and set off in search of subjects willing to be interviewed for a documentary on student homelessness.

Truth Be Told

My venture wasn't quite as simple as it sounds. I really had no idea what I was doing—about the filming process or about living in an RV. That's easy to admit now that I've got 15 years and a good amount of success under my tires. When I tell people about what I did, they give me a look like they'd give Mother Teresa, but I'm far from saintly.

The reality? I created a lean-and-mean organization, one woman. Me. I never had designs on expanding and we don't have a standard succession plan. No one would be crazy enough to do this!

I made it clear to my board of directors, all friends I've known for many years, I didn't want to be a "poverty pimp." Didn't want to get rich off the plight of the poor so we agreed on an adequate, but modest, salary. They've been a tremendous support in ways too numerous to mention. They've probably served much longer than expected, figuring I'd get tired of this nomadic existence years ago.

With their support, I knew it would be up to me to make HEAR US work from one day to the next. I had no idea how to do that. Our "success" is a tribute to countless individuals and organizations who helped along the way. My immediate focus was capturing stories of kids and parents in homeless situations, but my overall focus has always been changing the way our nation (mis)handles homelessness.

Bumpy Beginnings

As I left Illinois in my cumbersome vehicle/home/office in November 2005, I connected with Barbara Duffield. At the time Barbara worked for a national homelessness organization. She guided me to school districts across the country—in rural areas, resort communities, small towns, and mid-sized cities. She linked me with homeless liaisons who then connected me with families willing to share their stories.

One big obstacle to my plan were school district policies for interviewing students. A lawyer-friend drafted a super simple release form for kids' parents to sign which satisfied most administrators. Because Barbara knew these liaisons, I would often get the red carpet treatment. I'd schedule a time and place to meet the kids and their story unfolded.

The interviews happened in all kinds of places—motel rooms, shelters, school offices, sidewalks, homes where families were staying, and church shelters—wherever made sense. I just went with the flow, camera in hand and eyes open. The incredible thing was how straightforward these kids were. I didn't have any interview tricks (or skills, for that matter). I basically asked them what school meant to them and what was it like to be homeless and went from there. I tried to listen like I never listened before. I promised them I'd do everything to share their stories far and wide. They knew they were speaking on behalf of the invisible masses who, like them, have no place to call home.

My basic pattern was to have an appointment set up, drive somewhere to stay that was close so I'd arrive on time, meet, and interview. If I was smart enough, I'd shoot supplemental footage, B-roll as those in the film business call it, before or after the interview. Then I'd move onto the next place. My drive time between interviews gave me a chance to decompress and recompress. I couldn't get over the vast number of kids in that situation, and ached for those who weren't being helped by anyone. My admiration for homeless liaisons soared. My dismazement about the extent of homelessness skyrocketed.

By the end of my first round of travel, I had made a 20,000 mile loop through 34 states. I interviewed 75 kids in 13 states from 7-years-old to 25. My interviewing skills improved as I went along. I had yet to learn how to not "step on" my interviewee's story – interrupting at inopportune moments. I was astounded at the level of personal sharing they did. I wasn't a skilled interviewer by any notion. I bent over backwards to be gentle when getting into what I knew as tender spots. What I had going for me was years of connections with families; carrying a trunk full of stories that broke my heart and fueled my fire. I guess these kids picked up on my passion for this issue and trusted me to do right by them.

No Know-How, No Plan

Way back in 2005, when I knew nothing about filmmaking or living in an RV, I had no idea what I had gotten into and no plan beyond the highway in front of me. I've been on the road, living full-time in my van ever since. Maybe by the time this book gets published I'll land somewhere permanently, but who knows? The thing is, I love what I do! I'm the only one I know who makes short (3-5 min.) and mid-sized (20 min.) videos of kids and parents sharing their thoughts on homelessness and education. From what I hear, these videos are useful.

I've made dozens of films, thanks to the partnership I serendipitously fell into with Dr. Laura Vazquez, a film professor at Northern Illinois University. Laura edited my first film, *My Own Four Walls*. The documentary featured kids talking about what it was like to be homeless and what school meant to them. Later,

Laura and I collaborated on an award-winning feature-length film shown on PBS: *on the edge: Family Homelessness in America*. In the process she taught me enough about filmmaking to make me dangerous, at least dangerous to those who neglect or profess ignorance about families experiencing homelessness. Laura also wanted to learn more about homelessness. We both came out ahead.

Being Connected from Afar

My leap into this unusual lifestyle coincided with the explosion of social media. I hopped reluctantly onto Facebook in 2007. Though I've questioned that move many times, given the multitude of flaws that jeopardize users' privacy and sanity, I've stuck with it. My nomadic lifestyle required attaining and maintaining a connection with people across the country. My network from my previous jobs included legislators, legislative staff, journalists, professors, educators, advocates, activists, shelter and agency staff, and influential community leaders. A bunch of families I knew from my shelter days, and new families with homelessness experience, also joined my Facebook tribe. Social media provided a way for me to maintain and grow this wabi-sabi network. The bonus of social media equity—I am able to keep in touch with families I've worked with way back in my shelter days.

As a one-woman organization with an ambitious mission, I had to be realistic about my involvement with the deep hole of social media. I've honed a vibrant Facebook presence, now more than 2,300 "friends" with ten related pages. I've tapped into various homeless family/youth networks. I'm personally known to many of their members because of my work within their states. I have a minimal presence on Twitter (reluctant but essential) and a respectable LinkedIn network. I've blogged on different platforms. I'm currently active on Medium.com. I was the first "homelessness expert" to speak to the editorial board of the esteemed Christian

Science Monitor. I've written a number of op-ed pieces, contributed to stories for local and national media. My FB friends include journalists working for both large and modest media outlets. They believe in what I'm doing and are willing to extend their influence when I ask.

I've met a handful of Facebook friends who kept up with my travels, and I've stayed in more than one new friend's driveway. Long-time friends, including some I went to grade school with, have opened their homes to me and have contributed to my efforts financially and otherwise. Probably my most treasured connection, one I've maintained more than 50 years, is Sister Paula. Sister Paula was my high school freshman English teacher, school librarian and mentor. Now in her mid-90s, I visit her when I'm in the Joliet area. She slips $25 into my hand for gas money: a most-treasured donation.

What a lucky woman I am!

My Alter Ego and Pal

While I primarily traveled alone, I did vary that standard when I met Pat LaMarche back in 2010 in Carlisle, PA. She had been a columnist for the Bangor Daily News and I happened to read one of her opinion pieces, fascinated. She was describing then-vice presidential candidate Sarah Palin whose debate performance left a little to be desired.

Pat got my attention with her description of Sarah's need to write answers on her hand. "See, if she had big hands, she could write more important stuff on them, like the banner featuring a child that I read about in a New York City subway this weekend, sponsored by the Coalition for the Homeless, that read, 'A record 16,000 will go to sleep homeless in NYC tonight.' Heck, if she could get really big hands, she might mention that millions of children are homeless in this nation of ours."

I was intrigued. Who is this Pat LaMarche? I didn't know that she was the Green Party candidate for Vice President in 2004, and ran for Maine governor a couple of times, too. She ran homeless shelters. She's a mom of two amazing kids, not kids any more, but amazing nonetheless. And grandmother of two who will be famous someday, perhaps for their unmatched ability to memorize Shakespeare before they've learned to read. Pat's life partner, Chad, is a great match for her and a talented and wonderful guy.

When I emailed her and we realized that our kindred spirit paths might have crossed for some reason, I made my way up to Carlisle from DC and the rest was herstory.

We concocted an irregular itinerary of poverty/homelessness treks to different part of the country, starting with Southern Discomfort Tour in 2011. We would line up presentations, using the *My Own Four Walls* documentary to shine a light on the issue of kids being homeless. We'd visit shelters and encampments, arrange media interviews and write blogs. We'd meet and challenge elected officials whenever possible. We'd unleash our considerable creativity and passion to raise awareness about the injustice of poverty and homelessness.

We dubbed ourselves the *Babes of Wrath* in 2013, a moniker made permanent by Cenk Uygur when he interviewed us on *The Young Turks*, the Current TV news show filmed in LA. We were completing a weeks-long tour. We'd followed Rt. 66, the road leading to the promised land for the Okies as John Steinbeck poignantly wrote about in *Grapes of Wrath*. Over the years we've done several other tours. Our specialty—our creative or at least direct approach to call attention to this overlooked issue.

We continue to conspire as the Babes of Wrath. Be forewarned.

Building My Street Cred

During my copious coddiwompling, I've met countless people—homeless, those working with families/youth experiencing homelessness, public officials, do-gooders, and ordinary citizens. Some offered me the opportunity to park and plug into their homes, offices, or public facilities.

My willingness to create documentaries focused on family/youth homelessness within specific states has proven to be invaluable. My films help the states' homeless education efforts raise awareness. The filming process lets me take the pulse of homelessness and poverty in a variety of areas across the country. In addition to these contracted projects, I've done several freelance film projects. These are all available on my HEAR US website and through my video pages on Vimeo and YouTube. They're all listed in the appendix at the end of this book. Hundreds of thousands of views by thousands of subscribers have helped spread those stories far and wide.

Years ago, I decided to line up a Google search for topics like homeless students, homeless families, homeless children. Each morning I go first to these stories, skimming headlines and reading the more newsworthy accounts. Thanks to social media, I fling them onto my Facebook page, and occasionally Twitter, thinking of myself as "Diane Downer."

This regular early morning exercise is meaningful for me in many ways. I am amazed by how many places I've already traveled to and filmed. I can sometimes spot developments that need the attention of local officials or my national advocate friends. I get inquiries from my media FB friends and relish their coverage of a seemingly obscure topic – just because they saw it on my page. I identify places I should stop, when feasible, because they're doing something good or bad. I gauge trends—positive and negative—that help me in my film projects. My morning reflection of news about kids and families with no place to call home, dire and inspiring, gives me a perspective that helps me get through the day.

I've presented at state and national conferences. I use those appearances to promote my unique efforts to raise awareness about families and youth experiencing homelessness.

Having an extensive selection of videos, I've screened them at events across the country. My favorite presentation opportunities are at colleges, universities, and other educational institutions. My *Crossing the Line* book caught the attention of Dr. Marcus Redding, a law/social work instructor at Columbia University School of Social Work in New York City. Over the years, Marcus has connected me with his amazing students. Many knew little about homelessness and advocacy. He gave me a perfect arena to share my work. I've presented to hundreds of young people there over the years, and I've learned how to travel into NYC with ease!

I've gotten to know articulate, courageous spokespersons willing to share about their experiences of homelessness. I am often called upon to connect media professionals with someone willing to go public about their situation. This has led to national and international news coverage for me and, more importantly, those mired in the under-covered issue of family homelessness.

To be sure, I've stepped on the toes of shelter directors, legislators, school administrators and staff, and countless others along my travels. Without apology. I don't tolerate lawbreakers when it comes to the McKinney-Vento Homeless Education Act. I'm relentless. I'll fight to my last breath when I am asked to stand up for the rights of a kid being kept out of school or for a family getting the "bum's rush" by unenlightened school administrators.

Perhaps my biggest challenge is not becoming overly involved in the dire situations I encounter—a journalist's no-no. I've maintained a balance that stops me from emptying my personal account (or my organization's check book) to "save" a family from disaster. My compromise? I've always tried to connect the family in need with some legitimate help. On occasion I've broken my rule and helped out. But I know I'd never get down the road to my next interview if I don't rein in my impulse to fix.

The other concern I've had along the way is maintaining my integrity—personal and professional. From my days of teaching and running shelters, I know it's perilous to get into a position that can be misinterpreted in any kind of way. I assiduously work to not take advantage of someone's vulnerability. On a handful of occasions, I've sensed a subject's discomfort and extracted them from the process, hopefully with their self-esteem intact. A few times where I doubted the story, I checked it out and decided to scrap it. I have tried to not promise what I can't deliver. I show up. That's the most important first step, even when I didn't know what I was doing.

Dismazed and Driven

What fuels me? As long as I can remember, I've taken the side of the underdog. Knowing so many people who have gone through devastating experiences that caused, among other things, loss of housing, infuriates me. Often the circumstances surrounding homelessness reflects a huge gap in sensible policies and practices. Or the way they were treated registers off the charts of humanity, in a harmful way. Or they've been dealt a bad hand, bad beyond belief.

I've had family members who have experienced homelessness. It's real to me.

In 2014, after an outrageous news story snapped my last nerve, I coined the word *dismaze*, reflecting my perpetual state of dismay and amazement. Disgusted. Amazed. Amazed was too positive. It didn't take long for me to concoct "dismaze." I defined dismazed as "to dismay and overwhelm, to perplex with negative connotations, to really annoy the snot out of, typically because of blatant stupidity or gross insensitivity…"

During the past three decades, especially the last 15 years, I've gotten to know countless families. They have opened their hearts to me, courageously responding to my request to share their stories of loss, hardship, hopes and dreams. From them I've learned a lot. I promised them I'd share their stories far and wide. This is me keeping that promise.

Whatever you want to do,
just do it...
Making a damn fool of
yourself is absolutely
essential.

- Gloria Steinem

CHAPTER 2
Learning Curve

Going from tent-camping to even thinking of living in a recreational vehicle (RV) was a bigger leap than I could have imagined. Add to that adjustment my need to figure out the basics of filmmaking with a crew of one—me.

First steep learning curve—what kind of RV should I get? I'd like to say I researched and compared all the possibilities, but I didn't. I tried, but I might as well have been looking into which rocket ship I'd take to the moon. Cost was my major concern.

This part of my adventure, the purchase of the vehicle that would be my home for an unknown duration, was coming out of my pocket. Fortunately, the sale of my townhome in 2005 came just before the real estate bubble blew apart. I at least came out with a bit of unexpected cash. I had a garage sale to get rid of stuff. Renting a storage unit wasn't an option. This was my first reality check on my relationship with stuff.

I had no idea how long my endeavor might last. The answer was tied to whether HEAR US would have funds to pay me a modest salary and to cover my basic expenses. The July 1, 2005, birth of HEAR US, our nonprofit entity supporting this venture, was a leap. I've been in the nonprofit arena for long enough to know the basics. Basic #1 is having enough money to carry out your mission. That was a work in progress. With me as the only paid employee, it was just my job on the line. I am frugal by nature, and now was the time to be even more so.

This huge leap into the unknown, no matter how excited I was about my new mission, left me sad about what this meant to my life. Not having a home—I had no idea what that meant. I was about to find out.

My personal budget allowed for a payment of about $500 a month for my RV. Don't follow my path when it comes to making $60,000 purchases. All I knew was I needed to make a decision. I needed something not too big, not too expensive, and reliable.

I picked up my new RV, a 27' *Gulfstream Yellowstone* in early November 2005. I stood shell-shocked and numb as Tim, my RV instructor from the dealership, shared that he had been homeless a few years back. Whatever else he said was lost on me.

I packed my stuff into this tiny home on wheels under a cloud of inadequacy. Inadequate space. Inadequate knowledge of what I'd really need for my home, my office, my vehicle. What would I need? What tools? What office supplies? What clothing? For what seasons? What technology? How much food storage? What RV-related stuff? Hoses, electrical cords, etc.? I was utterly clueless and thoroughly stressed.

Other start-up issues that perplexed me:

The logistics of how to get mail. Since HEAR US needed a mailing address, I rented a box at a UPS store owned by friends/volunteers from my shelter days. They were enormously supportive and encouraging. My friend Helen, also our board treasurer, would check my business and personal mail and make that work. Strangely enough, it has.

Vehicle Name. The name "Tillie." When I started my adventure and bought my first vehicle, I needed a name so I wouldn't end up always saying "my RV." It became apparent that the vehicle was like a turtle. I'd pick up with all my belongings and lumber down the road. Like a turtle. Tillie was a name that didn't seem common. The last thing I'd want was to name a bulky, slow object after a friend. I didn't know any Tillies. Thus, I dubbed my rigs (I've now had two) Tillie the Turtle. In 2014, Tillie2, (T2) a 24' Sprinter van, replaced Tillie1, a 27' camper.

Signage. I wanted people to know that I was a woman on a mission, not just another RVer. A friend designed our first logo. A friendly sign company pulled strings to make that image into decals. They made it happen in time and at a cost I could afford as I scrambled to get Tillie1 ready to roll. Since that first imprint, the signage has changed. It's now much improved with our Charlie logo. I got smart with Tillie2 and got magnetic signs.

Money. When I first concocted this scheme, I knew I'd need money. How much? I had no idea. My plan was we'd sell the video I made on my first cross-country trip. Proceeds from my book, *Crossing the Line: Taking Steps to End Homelessness*, would be plowed back into our treasury. Speaking engagements, donations, maybe grants (though foundations don't tend to fund unconventional projects such as this), and what else? I had no clue.

When I told my restaurant owner-friends Betsy and Francois who had been shelter volunteers about my idea, they offered their establishment, staff, food and incredible hospitality to me. We could have a dinner. We could invite up to 75 people (their capacity) and charge whatever we wanted. The rest was up to us. If I needed an omen, which I did, this was it! Our dinner was a wonderful event and we raised $7,000 to get me on the road.

A local foundation also stepped up with a grant of $5,000 for the equipment I needed. A good friend and her husband have kicked in significantly over the years, making my life a lot easier.

A couple of noteworthy events have also helped. My longtime idol, Peter Yarrow, of Peter, Paul and Mary fame, did a concert for our 10th Anniversary. Another favorite, beloved musician, George Winston, has done three fundraising concerts for us.

Repeat and one-time donors have also supported HEAR US. I've managed to line up speaking engagements and film projects which also kept me rolling.

Nonprofit status. A lawyer friend got it started, and others jumped on board. Before long HEAR US Inc. was a bonafide nonprofit. Until the official approval came through, Bridge Communities, a respected nonprofit that provides transitional housing to families in DuPage County, served as our fiscal sponsor enabling our donors receive tax-deductions.

Board of Directors. I knew I needed a special group of people to oversee and support this unique and exciting organization. I needed people I could trust even though I wasn't attending in-person at board meetings. They needed to trust me. I hand-picked a cadre of wonderful women and one man, all of whom I've known for decades. They jumped at the opportunity, another huge source of encouragement for me. Most of them are still involved and supportive these 15 years later.

Miscellaneous. Other details—communication technology, banking, internet access, etc.—all tumbled into place. It's mind-blowing to look back at the primitive, expensive technology we used in the beginning.

Hit the Road! Learning Curves: Round 2

In mid-November 2005, when I drove out of Naperville with freshly-applied signage making my HEAR US mission official, I wasn't excited. I was fearful. As in "what the hell did I just do?" fearful. My fears weren't assuaged. My first clueless night "boon-docking" (parking without being plugged in) I chose what I hoped to be a safe spot, a lot between a Holiday Inn and Denny's in Indianapolis. I did what I read about—I covered the windows, locked the doors, and went to sleep.

I awoke early and decided to avail myself of Denny's coffee and breakfast instead of making my own in my intimidating little kitchen space. As I stepped into the parking lot, I had to avoid a gushing flow of water underneath my rig. What??? I went into Denny's and tried to casually inquire about the river. The hostess indifferently replied that their water main had broken in the middle of the night.

I hastily assessed the possibilities, and figured that none of the workers could wash their hands. My normally non-squeamish self quickly turned around and hightailed it out of the parking lot before it might turn into a big sinkhole swallowing my new vehicle. I ended up pulling into a rest area and made my own coffee and breakfast. I naively marveled at the convenience of the generator that powered my toaster.

Even though I was new to driving that humongous vehicle, I opted to get off of the boring interstate in Kentucky and take secondary roads as far as I could. I was on my way to my first stop in Atlanta. I had to become adept at handling the monstrosity or things would get ugly, and dangerous. In the fashion of "lean into it," I wended my way through the backroads of Kentucky and Tennessee, getting a grip on using the side mirrors as my "eyes" since my rearview mirror was moot. A windstorm with 70-mph gusts provided another learning opportunity.

My journey south to the Atlanta area was, in part, to visit my parents for Thanksgiving. My HEAR US journey would officially start right after the holiday. My family's encouragement and support mollified my private second-guessing of this vague, ambitious venture.

Rules and Skills for RVers

My learning curve was filled with rules/protocols and skills to learn, mostly about the world of RVing. Among them:

- Rule 1 of RVing. Many places don't allow people to sleep in their vehicles. My parents' retirement community didn't but they made an exception after the fact.
- Rule 2. Watch my (Tillie's) butt. Don't knock off mailboxes. I did.
- Skill 1. Parking requires spatial awareness, especially when extra items, like a bike/bike rack make your vehicle even bulkier. See Rule 2.
- Skill 2. Dumping. Using the plumbing—sink and bathroom—creates waste water. I had to find the appropriate place to dispose of it. I could write an entire book about my dumping experiences. Suffice to say this task scared the crap out of me, but I needed to develop this skill quickly. The nearby campground provided my first lesson. I invited my youngest sis, Patty, to join me, knowing we'd have lots of giggles. But she snuck out leaving me on my own. I managed to get it done, not textbook-style, I'm sure.

Other Critical Lessons on the Road

I was impatient to hit the road, but waited until the infamous Atlanta area rush-hour traffic cleared Monday after Thanksgiving. My backroads route would take me through Alabama on my way to Louisiana, my next first stop. Dad urged me to wait, as a band of nasty weather was headed our way. But even as an adult-child I didn't listen. He called that afternoon and offered to pay for a hotel room (I was pretty broke at this point). "Thanks, Dad, I've got this."

It was a bit disconcerting when – as I was ineptly getting settled into the Alabama state park – the tornado siren went off. That was my first "camping" site, so I had no idea what a person in an RV did about the basics, much less the protocol on tornado warnings. I stuck my head out and saw other campers scurrying towards the concrete bathhouse. I followed, wishing my cellphone was charged. A handful of us from across the country hunkered down for over an hour before the all-clear sounded.

My take on this exciting experience? I'd give myself a D- on storm preparedness. I needed a better flashlight. I needed to have a good raincoat ready somewhere. My cell phone should have been charged. And I learned to close the damn windows (which fortunately didn't drench the inside too badly) and to close the slide-out (the movable part of an RV that slides out to make more room) to minimize awning damage.

It was an interesting, humbling initiation to life on the road. I envisioned explaining to my folks that I'd need help because my camper blew into the lake. It didn't. That was as close to disaster as I wanted to get. But others followed.

Other Lessons Facing Me

The many aspects of RVing were daunting. I eventually learned the basics of hooking up to the campground electric and water, campground etiquette, what all the gauges and buttons meant. I learned to monitor supplies of propane and water. I learned the hard way not to drive under low-hanging branches or other obstacles. I acquired parallel parking skills. I mastered toll-booth rules, and more. In addition to these essentials, I had to fast-track my technical skills and know-how.

Tech equipment. My video camera, for instance. When I finally stopped driving long enough to take a look at my new professional-grade video camera, I was flabbergasted at all the buttons, knobs, and places to plug things in that I had no clue about. And that was for starters.

Internet connection. Hard to remember the primitive days of cell phones and mobile internet access, but my journal clearly indicated that I had more of a problem with these things than I remember. Remember the "air card"? Neither do I. But it had to be plugged into a computer and would, if you were lucky, give a signal for the phone and internet access. If it worked.

Power. My first vehicle didn't have solar panels. Unless I was hooked up to shore power (a landline—plugged in) I couldn't power my laptop. Without that working, my air card didn't work. And it didn't work plenty of times based on my log review. I had a generator (genny) on my first rig which produced electricity for me but cost money because it used gasoline. Fuel prices rose above $2 per gallon just as I set out in my gas-hog of a vehicle (about 10 mpg). I couldn't be frivolous about firing up genny.

Navigation. In those pre-smartphone days, navigation was another source of extreme frustration. My first GPS (global positioning system) cost about $500 and didn't work. I returned it. Other efforts to find my way required a working internet connection, which was far from the norm. My atlas usually got me to the general location but lacked specifics. I ended up driving around a lot. I would look for Walmart or the campground to park in or to find my filming location and bemoan the wasted fuel. Cha-ching! Technology has come a long way!

Still, my first worries were more related to survival.

Waste Tanks. If you're squeamish, you'll be forgiven for skipping this. I'll not go into the grossest details, but I can't write about this essential topic without mentioning some unmentionables. In mobile home life, we become acutely aware of the process of waste.

"Waste" refers to what goes down our sinks, showers and toilets. "Finite" is a relevant, related concept. Grey and black water tanks only provide so much storage, so you have to "dump." Dumping is done in dump stations. I now have an app that lists those spots. Before that app, it was a challenge to figure out where to dump, preferably free. I remember the first time I had to pay $10 to dump. It was worth it considering the alternative.

My first rig had a gauge to tell me when things were getting full (waste tanks) and empty (water supply). I soon became skeptical of gauges. Inaccurate, due to the accumulation of stuff on the sensors. I'll let it go at that. My approach became dump and fill whenever I could because I never knew when the next opportunity would be available. I think that's a good mantra for life.

A classic example of my nightmare dump experience: I had business in the northeast part of the country—New York City, Carlisle, PA, and Washington DC, in January and February 2016. Winter. Flawed planning but I had no choice.

Heading up that way in Tillie2 (T2), I tried taking care of business, filling my water tank and emptying my waste tanks. But for a bunch of reasons this wasn't possible. I switched to survival mode, using resources as frugally as possible.

First stop, NYC. Fortunately, I've discovered the ease of NYC visits. Directly across from Manhattan, the Walmart in Secaucus, NJ has a big lot. New Jersey transit buses stop there before heading to the Port Authority in Times Square. Their cheap fare makes this a great arrangement. It was cold when I locked up

Tillie2 and headed out. When I need to be there more than one night, I have friends in the City who let me sleep at their place instead of forking over hundreds for a hotel room.

Yes, I did worry about my rig sitting in New Jersey. The temps dropped, which worried me more than anything. With good reason. After presenting at a conference the next day, I hopped the bus to get back to my little house on wheels. It had been below freezing the night before, so I wasn't surprised to find the water pump frozen. Not good. That meant other things were frozen, too.

I headed to my friend Pat LaMarche's (aka Babe of Wrath) in Carlisle, PA for an extended visit, about a 4-hour drive. I had a film screening scheduled. Plus, I had agreed to film a short documentary about the elderly folks from the shelter that she ran. She wanted me to show what life was like for them, especially in this bitter cold. I was able to park at the shelter's resource center. I had to work my parking around the movements of a crowd of people being transported to and from the nightly shelter site. But that was fine because, after they left, I was able to plug in and hug my heater.

When I landed in Carlisle, both my water supply tank and my waste tanks were frozen. This was a big issue. The temps were not showing any mercy. To make matters worse, a major snowstorm was barreling our way. I'll just say I did everything possible to alleviate the problem. The water pump needed a fuse, which I handled. The waste tanks, well, that was another story. A friend arranged for me to park inside the heated garage at the fire department for several hours. I was able to put a heater on the affected area. A firefighter who has an RV and understood the essence of my problem tried everything he could to help. Nothing worked. I ended up buying a portable camp potty. I hunkered down, parked at the shelter for the blizzard. The storm, dubbed *Snowzilla,* deposited two feet of snow on the area.

By the time it stopped snowing, my rig was an igloo, totally encased. I stayed warm because I'd plugged in. The guys staying at the shelter dug me out. My temporary solutions got me through the storm.

My filming and screening went well, but I was happy to head south. My next stop was DC, only a couple hours away. I purchased an auger and took care of what ailed Tillie. I knew I wasn't done with winter trials. And now every time I'm in freezing temps I'm traumatized. Really. I skipped the gross details. Use your imagination. The Winter of 2016 is etched in my psyche.

Not lost on me? My relative comfort compared to the people relying on the shelter for a place to sleep. Few outside the homelessness world realize how brutal life is for those with nowhere to live. For the documentary I made for Pat, I spent time filming Cindy and Dave in their hideaway. They hung out at an abandoned gas station where they had shaped a cubby hole to escape the weather. They cobbled together their version of *the comforts of home*. They had a place they could sit, nap, read or just exist during the daytime hours. It wasn't lost on me the difference between their discomfort and mine. No room for complaining on my end.

Temperature Matters

I confess to having taken creature comforts for granted, like heat and cooling.

Cold weather presents a conundrum. Tillie1 had a furnace that used propane from the storage tank built into my vehicle. It also required power—shore power (plugging into an electrical outlet) or genny. Genny required expensive gasoline. The heater sucked enormous quantities of the finite amount of propane that I also needed to fuel the refrigerator/freezer (never really understood that concept) and give me hot water.

The finite amount of propane was an issue I needed to respect, especially in winter. Propane was hard to find in certain areas. Cold air poured into Tillie1 with a vengeance. The RV's insulation was inadequate at best. Since I didn't manage to do what other RVers do—head to warmer climes during winter—I paid the price. Running the furnace meant using up the propane at a rate that quickly depleted my tank. I learned that having a small portable heater was the smart thing to do, but that required electricity which wasn't always a given.

In early April 2007, I landed at a state park in western Iowa. It would have been a great spot except that the high temps were in the 20s and the wind chill knocked it down to zero. Cold air poured in through every orifice. I had the furnace on full blast, to little avail. I was frickin' freezing! It was Easter weekend, which meant places that sold propane were closed just about the time my reserves ran out. To add to the "fun," the electrical power would go off for a few moments, then resume. Disconcerting! The intermittent electric, empty propane tank, plus my frozen and full dump tank, combined to change my plans. I could not stay in that park for several days. I pulled the plug and headed east to my DuPage County, Illinois hideaway.

For sure, the arctic blast challenges were the most daunting; followed closely by the heat waves.

Hot weather. The AC unit on my first rig sounded like a helicopter sitting on my roof. So, I never used it after my first time. Instead I relied on the pretty amazing Fantastic Fans™ that pulled an impressive amount of air through roof vents. I decided that sweating was good for me. I got used to warmer temps. I learned to put my dark chocolate bars in the fridge.

Since I stubbornly refused to use Tillie1's AC, I had to figure out where I could park with my windows open and fans blowing at night. During the day I'd spend time in libraries, Starbucks, Panera, or other places where I could stay cool and work. It was inconvenient, but doable. Nighttime heat was pretty miserable a few times, but it obviously didn't kill me.

Staying cool at night became a little easier with Tillie2. If I parked somewhere I felt safe, I'd open the back doors and welcome the breeze. Lucky me, a few times it's been possible to back up to the ocean or a river. The screens keep the little critters out. I accept that the big critters—people with no business coming in—theoretically could intrude. But I hope not. I figure sleeping in a tent, with paper-thin fabric separating the camper from the outside—an experience I know well—is also theoretically dangerous.

One thing that these temperature challenges gave me was a minuscule sense of what folks go through when they lack access to creature comforts I take for granted. It's one thing for a white, middle-age, semi-respectable looking (ha!) woman to hang out in a library, cafe or other quasi-public place for hours. Someone who lacks access to hygiene and clean clothes, without money to be a paying patron faces barriers that I don't. Someone with behavior issues that make it hard to hang around without disturbing others? Well, they often get the bum's rush. Their options are limited on a good day, especially when access to bathrooms is factored in. I figure I had it made, maybe not in the shade because often that too was lacking.

Friends Everywhere

My friend Cynthia Martinez, the much-loved and indomitable homeless liaison for Wichita, Kansas School District

259, urged me to come by during their 8-week summer Camp IBA—Imagine, Believe, Achieve. In June 2015, I headed down to spend a week in Wichita, sleeping in the downtown parking lot of the Salvation Army. I filmed and photographed their most wondrous summer camp for kids experiencing homelessness. Few things could get me to go anywhere in Kansas in the summer. Temps hover in the 90+ degree range. My little tin can of a house is not made for that kind of heat, especially when I can't open up all the doors and windows at night.

All I can say is it was worth every sweaty night! This experience for the 125-175 campers could not have been more enriching! They learned to play guitars and drums. They worked on academic skills. They created amazing art projects. They frolicked in a refreshing pool. They hiked and explored at a nearby nature center. And more! I was exhausted! I filmed and photographed every joyful moment I could, and was able to produce short videos that were shared with the entire group.

In what I find to be a quirky perk of my lifestyle, I pull the threads of my friendships to arrange lodging. I often stay with a dear friend in Scottsdale, Arizona when I'm in that part of the country. Turns out she has a friend who has a sister who is the director of the family shelter at the Wichita Salvation Army. Voila! A place to stay. Not only did she welcome me for that week of filming Camp IBA, but she "babysat" for T2 for three weeks while I filmed in Hawaii in 2018. As my sister says, I've got friends everywhere!

Flying or Driving?

My confidence in my driving ability has been tested multiple times during this adventure. Other than stupid minor scrapes, oddly enough all on the right (passenger) side of my vehicles, I've not had an accident. I hope I didn't just jinx myself!

My first year on my sojourn tossed a few doozies at me. Etched in my memory is one drive across I-80 in Nebraska. Crosswinds pummeled me the entire way. I had to hang onto the steering wheel with both hands, not even able to scratch my nose. Driving my high-profile vehicle with crosswinds, or headwinds, was exhausting. Tailwinds worked great. They improved fuel efficiency.

Another hair raising experience also happened in my first year. I was headed down to Texas on Rt. 75. The wide-open 4-lane highway had signs that implied "Let 'er rip" with their 75 mph speed limit. So, I did. Traffic was light. I was on the phone with a friend. All of a sudden, I felt a massive jerk on the steering. I saw the strangest sight out of my right sideview mirror. The awning on the passenger side, a 12' long structure that was supposed to be securely rolled up had unfurled like a wing. One wing is worse than 2 wings. Grateful that no one was next to me, I brought Tillie1 in for a landing along the roadside. I pondered my next step. The huge piece of canvas was torn and the roller that had held it up was dangling like a broken limb.

Nothing prepared me for this challenge. I stood there staring at this scene when a pickup truck pulled behind me. A big bubba got out and walked my way. My stereotype maker was in full gear. Then this giant of a Texan, a preacher who called himself Rev. Pat, asked if I needed any help. To say "no" would have been an obvious lie. So, I said, "yes." He took a look then asked me to drive his truck alongside my injured vehicle. He tossed me the keys and I clambered in his massive pickup, with his bible riding shotgun, and he hopped in the back. While standing in the bed of his pickup, he whipped out a big knife to amputate the remains of the awning. I eased his red pickup alongside my wounded vehicle as he surgically removed the afflicted wing. His plan worked and made more sense than my plan of climbing on top of T1 and leaning over the edge with a Swiss Army knife to do the same thing.

When he was finished, I bundled up the remains and shoved them inside my rig. "Thank you, Rev. Pat. I hardly knew ya." I regretted my unspoken judgments about that bible-toting reverend in an oversized pickup truck. He did the job and didn't ask for my soul in return.

My vehicle was still covered by the warranty. I was happy when the manufacturer replaced the awning, which I never used again.

Size Matters

I never felt at ease when driving Tillie1 in narrow spots. And the right side of my vehicle showed it. The fold-out steps always got mangled. I replaced them at least 4 times, at $400 a pop. They'd grind on a curb and eventually get twisted beyond repair.

The worst was going over those skinny suspension bridges. The anxiety I'd feel in my gut increased with every second I was on a bridge. I had flashbacks to when I was about 17 and had to drive my four younger siblings from our home in Pompano Beach, Florida to Key West to meet up with my parents for a holiday weekend.

I had Mom's big fat Chrysler station wagon which I swore was 10 feet wide. To make matters worse, I had just gone to the eye doctor and my pupils were dilated. Sunny Florida. Car full of kids. Lots of narrow bridges, including the famed Seven Mile Bridge, all the way down to the southernmost tip of the United States. I guess that was good training.

Because I drove to the same parts of the country several times, I'd try to pick a different route without going too far out of my way. In July 2010, I headed south from Illinois on Rt. 45 which offered an interesting look at rural parts of the state (OK, it's mostly cornfields) once I got past the Chicago suburbs.

About the time I reached the Ohio River, after an exciting stop in Metropolis, Illinois, home of my childhood idol, Superman, I was a bit tired. I could have taken the big ol' I-24 bridge but, no, I stuck with Rt. 45. That meant driving across a frightening 10-span truss bridge, the Brookport Bridge. It's a 2-lane narrow structure that seemed to shrink width-wise as I inched my way across. An eternity. About halfway over, I whacked my right side mirror on the bridge, essentially knocking my right "eye" out. The mirror, which stuck out like a Dumbo ear before I mangled it, flapped and clunked against the side of my beleaguered vehicle. I did manage to get across the rest of the way. I pulled into a parking lot to assess the damage.

Bad. Without that mirror, I can't see anything on my right side, so I couldn't go far without getting it fixed. To the nearest Ford dealership I went. Fortunately, Paducah, KY was right there. The service guy was very helpful and ordered the parts to be shipped overnight. All totaled, that bridge set me back a budget-busting $700. Ouch. Spent the night in a "Camp Walmart" parking lot, aka my freebie place to park overnight. I was able to get back on the road the next afternoon.

I Don't Belong Here

Parking, especially overnight, can be easy or impossible, or anywhere in-between. Signs warning of towing are ubiquitous. Camp Walmart is famous for having signs that read "No RV Overnight Parking" but the lots tend to be filled with RVs (except in the winter when I'm one of the only ones silly enough to be there). This contributes to what I think is "sign immunity." We learn to believe the worst will not happen if we break the rules.

I'm not a fan of Atlanta but, since I have 2 brothers and several friends there, I do end up going there more often than I'd like. In December 2014, I drove to my brother's condo to have dinner. It was a Sunday night so the parking lot adjacent to his condo was pretty empty. A small strip mall had a pizza joint that was open. The rest of the businesses were dark, so I wasn't going deprive any customers of a space. I did see the sign threatening illegal parkers with the boot, but how would someone know I wasn't there to eat pizza?

As I left Tillie2, a pickup truck coasted to a stop near me and the driver opened his window and said I'd be booted if I parked there. *What? Who are you?* I didn't want to get into a brawl of words. I nodded and walked on, heading up to my brother's for dinner.

We came out for a "Tillie Tour" a few hours later. A yellow device clamped to my front passenger tire got our attention. Booted. Damn!

Evidently booting is rampant in Atlanta, and probably other cities too. It's a sweet gig for tow truck companies. No due-process to thwart their over-vigilant booting. $75 to the tow truck driver to get freed. I get it. Illegal parking can be problematic. But if every private parking lot has these vultures lurking, and no public parking is available, what's a person to do?

I felt violated. It was late and I was tired. I said goodbye to my family and headed to the nearest Camp Walmart, which also had a sign threatening illegal parkers. I bet on the reluctance of Walmart to alienate customers. That night I got lucky. But the feeling of vulnerability lingers. My dislike of being in Atlanta went up a few notches.

My Filming Learning Curves

Looking back, my challenges with filming were different, but as daunting, as driving.

My first round, where I interviewed 75 kids in 13 states for the film that ended up being named *My Own Four Walls*, I had lots to learn. Having never done any video work before, my knowledge gap was seismic. Good thing I operate well in that mode. It's also a good thing friends stepped forth when I needed them.

My friend Tom Parisi, a former Aurora Beacon News reporter who covered social issues when I was running the shelter there, moved over to Northern Illinois University around the time I embarked on my HEAR US project. He kept up with me thanks to my humble newsletter. He read that I needed help with video editing. He connected me with Laura Vazquez. What a gift!

When I returned from my first round of travel in the summer of 2006 with more than 50 hours of video footage, I thought *OK, now what?* I asked around. I went to visit a guy whose business was film editing. He was nice. I knew he did this for a living, but when he tossed me the figure of $10,000, I almost passed out! Having done a significant amount of film editing since those days, I can understand why someone would deserve that much. But I didn't have ten grand to fork out, so Plan B, Tom's connection.

I set up an appointment with Professor Vazquez and headed out to Northern Illinois University (NIU) with a box full of video tapes. I was totally clueless about what I was asking. Laura, who has produced many award-winning documentaries over her long career, received me kindly. She took a look at some of the video clips. She agreed to work with me on the production compiling those interviews. For nothing! We agreed that her students could do this as a class project with her oversight and my input. What a great arrangement!

My first lesson? I had stepped on my interviews. The kids would be talking and I'd talk over them. Often. I wish I had met my video guru, Laura, before I left on that first journey. She schooled me a-plenty in the art of making a documentary. Fortunately, my interviewees said enough good things that I didn't step on. She and her student team could salvage sufficient clips.

Lesson 2. B-roll. I didn't know what that was. And I didn't realize how important it was. These are the scenes a filmmaker inserts to keep viewers interested, not just staring at the interview subject. B-roll conceals edits. It can also cover wonky video, which I had in abundance. I sat in on Laura's documentary-making class in the fall of 2006 where I learned a lot.

Lesson 3. Steady camera. I'm not a fan of tripods. But I recognize that keeping the camera steady is important. I use a monopod. Laura would say not good enough, but better than nothing. Sometimes it's awkward to bring a big tripod, or even a monopod, to a filming location. I sometimes hand hold: as steady as possible.

Lesson 4. Microphone. For the first round of travel, I didn't figure out the microphone thing until the end. Instead, I relied on the camera's inadequate built-in mic. I'll just say that I'm grateful for the student who worked on the audio challenges my ineptitude created.

As the work progressed, I was awed at how powerful those kids I interviewed were. They spoke so poignantly about what school meant to them. They explained how homelessness affected them personally as well as how it impacted their school work. My inexperienced "style" made the film authentically organic in nature.

The students' editing and music brought it together in a way I could have only have done in my dreams! They finished *My Own Four Walls*, in March 2007.

Much of my time in the fall of 2006 was spent in the NIU film lab. A foreign experience for me, I became more comfortable as each session unfolded. Laura and I learned how to work together. Eventually she asked if I'd work with her on a feature-length film about family homelessness. Not knowing what I was saying yes to, I agreed.

I did, however, ask Laura why she wanted to make such a film. She explained that, as a 21-year-old wife and mother of a baby boy, she had an abusive spouse. She decided to pack up her baby, hop in her beater car, with little money, and head to California. She had friends willing to let her couch surf—double up—until she got back on her feet. Her homelessness as a young mother, her abilities as a documentarian, coupled with the chance to collaborate with me, fueled her desire to do the project.

We spent four years working on that documentary. I scouted potential subjects as I traveled. Laura taught me about filmmaking. I taught her about homelessness. She took a sabbatical and got grants. We traveled some places together. Sometimes we met up and filmed then she would fly back to Illinois. Our efforts were met by willing subjects. The end product, *on the edge: Family Homelessness in America*, an hour-long documentary, won film festival awards. It aired on PBS on Mother's Day, 2012.

My humble realization? My learning curves are present each day and I'm fortunate to have the wherewithal and good friends to help me meet those challenges.

If you tell the truth, you don't have to remember anything.

- Mark Twain

CHAPTER 3
Stealth Skills

Stealth noun - secret, clandestine, or surreptitious procedure; a furtive departure or entrance.
Dictionary.com

The Thing About Stealth

If you're not familiar with the world of homelessness, you probably don't grasp the importance of stealth. Besides the world of espionage, that I know nothing about, stealth when it comes to homelessness looms large. Most people, particularly elected officials, don't want to know that people have no place to call home. They ignore families lingering on the streets (or in any number of places they can find). Most families without homes don't want the officials to know they're lingering on the streets either. I guess that's how the term "malingering" originated.

Too Big to Hide

My 27' long, 10'4" high, 8'6" wide vehicle known as Tillie the Turtle, aka Tillie1, was too big to hide. The bright white body (except for most of the time when covered with road dirt) made a statement. Most of Tillie1's surface was covered with huge heart-stopping images of kids. They were photos I took at my friend Lesly's shelter back in DeKalb, Illinois. I was hoping to rip hearts out. I did have one woman pull up next to me at a stoplight, jump out, and toss a $20 in my open window.

The best stealth I could hope for with Tillie1 was no one bothering me when I slept where I shouldn't. From what I can remember, I had adequate privacy. From these early experiences, I thought I knew what I needed when I was ordering T2 in 2014.

Nowhere to Hide

My first attempt at stealth parking in my new van, Tillie2, was so pathetic it was laughable. I had just picked up that smaller, more fuel-efficient rig from the Austin, Texas, Sportsmobile in October 2014, and needed to hang around Austin to get a few things fixed.

I deliberately ordered the privacy curtain and shades, assuming that privacy meant more than not offering parking lot shadow shows in my windows. I wanted a total, no-one-knows-I'm-in-here black-out.

My customary, free, overnight parking option was the noisy "Camp Walmart" lot where shoppers, truckers, and loud motorcyclists regularly roared throughout the night. Since I had acquired an anonymous, classy vehicle, I decided to park in a quieter Austin motel parking lot, generally a no-no. Without Tillie1's blatant signage, I hoped that my dark blue, tinted-glassed, window-shaded Mercedes-Benz (MB) Sprinter van would be just another vehicle in the lot. I hoped I would sleep in peace, away from the raucous Camp Walmart lots.

Much to my chagrin, I discovered that my new shades were far from private. Anyone in the parking lot could see light inside, and shadows from my every movement. The privacy shades just kept viewers from unimpaired views, but alluring shadows blew my cover. I figured out a frugal, simple fix. I purchased a roll of mylar insulation. Easy to cut and fit to each window, I hoped to add an insulating layer to my little house. Better than tin foil! Eventually, a friend sewed a dark curtain to separate the driving cab from my living space. I was then totally stealth.

I've needed to refine my stealth mode. I occasionally parked where living in a vehicle was not allowed: like hotel parking lots when I'm at a conference. Stealth has served me well on university campuses, school parking lots, hospitals, shelters, hoity-toity neighborhoods, and in Mercedes-Benz lots. I've had to stop for service there far too many times.

My connection with Mercedes-Benz? I never would have chosen a Mercedes because of their reputation for high end.

My first vehicle, a Gulfstream Yellowstone 27' Class C RV, served me well except for fuel mileage (10 mpg). After 9 years in Tillie1, I decided to further downsize. I looked at Class B vehicles: vans efficiently outfitted with the comforts of home. My Mom passed away in 2013 and left each of us (me and my 3 siblings) a modest inheritance. Mom was a MB fan, which amused me because I had no use for such elitist brands. Never say never.

Scoffing at things, like I did for years about RVs and Mercedes-Benz, always comes back to haunt me. As a tent camper in my earlier years, I'd rant endlessly if I was stuck behind an RV. "That's not camping!" My work with impoverished folks also fueled my disdain for the affluence of brands like Mercedes.

So…

As I pondered the selection of Class B vans that got decent fuel mileage, the one that seemed to be the best choice was the MB Sprinter. I locked onto Sportsmobile, a company that converted vans into RVs. That's how I made my choice. Mom's money paid for my van which ended up costing about $100,000, a sum that caused me to gulp. I justified it in all kinds of ways. It was my house, my office and my vehicle. Three for the price of one. Not finding a buyer for Tillie1 in time, I ended up donating it to a friend's nonprofit organization. I said goodbye to this relatively trouble-free vehicle after 9 years.

The irony of my MB choice has smacked me in the face more times than I can count. Having spent my first decade of nomadic life in a vehicle that was overall trouble-free, I expected even better from my Sprinter. My dismazement with MB started in October 2014 in the first weeks I had the vehicle. While traveling in the middle of nowhere South Dakota, the "Check Engine" light started dancing on my dashboard. My "Check Engine" light experiences became my constant companion.

When Stealth Shatters

Money makes a difference. If my nice-looking vehicle is parked where it shouldn't be, I might be asked to move. A ratty-looking vehicle would likely be ticketed or towed. Sometimes the police get called. In the desert area abutting California's Joshua Tree National Park, a family pseudo-camping in their less-than stellar camper had a nightmare police visit in March, 2018.

While heading to southern California, I got the heads-up from a journalist friend about a homeless family that was split apart by child welfare authorities. The parents were put in jail and their 4 kids sent to foster homes, all because some nosy neighbor apparently didn't like the way the family was living. I wrote about it at the time.

From my Medium article dated 3/17/2018

The Joshua Tree family's pattern is all too typical. Their last rental housing was 4 years ago. Allegedly the owner died and heirs wanted Mona Kirk, Daniel Panico and their 3 kids out, so the family packed their belongings in plastic bins, rented storage

*units (common for many households), and
took refuge at property they owned in the
high desert adjacent to Joshua Tree National
Park.*

*Five-acre parcels of land come
cheap here, at least for now. Mona said she
bought the property years ago at an online
auction. Their plan was to build a dome
home, a project her science-minded husband
has been working on.*

*They stayed in their trailer,
eventually turning it over to their cats for
protection from the coyotes. The family
bounced around, staying with friends, in
vehicles, and a variety of places temporarily
available to them.*

I learned the family tried to mind their own business:
stealth living. They thought they'd be able to pursue their quirky
lifestyle, which included by all accounts, being wonderful parents. I
heard speculation about how this situation blew up into a major
deal. Likely a neighbor saw the kids crawling out of a 4'x 8' box
"shed" that they were sleeping in. News reports from a few months
earlier about a family roughly 90 miles away in southern California
who had locked their children in their house and abused them didn't
help. The police and child welfare representatives descended on the
Joshua Tree scene and it all went bad from there.

I spent several days in this area, getting a sense of the
family's story, talking to locals. I witnessed what the school district
saw when they dealt with their sizable population of homeless
students. What I learned was dismazing, both about Mona and

Daniel's situation as well as the entire district's homeless student conundrum.

First, about Mona and Daniel: I met with their lawyers. I sat in the courtroom. I spoke with several people who knew the family well. It appeared that the situation got out of control like a prairie wildfire. The steps to mitigate it were way out of proportion.

The family lost their housing but had creatively made do the best they could without asking for help. Would I suggest turning over their camper to protect their cats from coyotes? No. But I'm not a cat lover so my perspective is tainted. I love kids more so I wouldn't have suggested that the family be split up. That can traumatize kids. And parents, Mona and Daniel weren't abusing their children. They were decent, albeit unconventional, parents who made sure their kids had plenty of learning opportunities.

We don't tolerate unusual people well, especially if they lack resources. Fortunately, the locals rallied behind this family and raised a ton of money, enough to buy and renovate a house for them. Parents and kids were reunited months after this fiasco. Kudos to the local effort.

An interesting side note that I was not aware of before spending time in Joshua Tree. A high number of affordable houses were flipped into the profitable vacation rental market, leaving previous tenants house-less, and in many cases homeless. Many renters couldn't afford to pay the increasing rates as the area's housing shifted to accommodating tourists. The school district lost hundreds of families to this trend. Hundreds of students became homeless, doubled up, when their family homes got ripped out from under them by this change in the housing market.

Even the tiny homesteading cabins built en masse 50 or so years ago were being tossed into the vacation rental fray. The cleverest I saw was a lot that used old boats—a cabin cruiser and a sailboat—for tourists. At least they weren't depleting the sparse existing housing.

Stealth in the Land of Mickey

Another not so obvious stealth trend is found in the motel industry. I saw it a-plenty in the Disney World region during a pass through the Orlando area in 2012. You might think motels = tourists. Some tourists do stay in motels. But from what I've seen in many parts of the country, families and single individuals who lose housing often turn to, and get stuck in, motels. Some McKinney-Vento liaison friends in the counties surrounding Disney World opened my eyes to what was a shocking level of stealth homelessness. What was stealth about it? The tourist industry would never want visitors to know that they were staying in what boiled down to be a 21st century homeless shelter.

Not Just Another Tourist

I met Chris as he was hunting for an empty cart to move his family's stuff. They had landed at the motel four years before we met. His story was like so many I've heard that I could almost recite it before being told. He, his wife Carolina, and their baby lost their housing when he lost his job, as the real estate and job market bubbles burst. They put their stuff in storage. That $200 monthly expense made sense in the beginning of their homeless-honeymoon. But soon after that budget-busting expense was beyond their ability to pay. Their storage unit was padlocked and their things sold and/or tossed. Important documents, pictures, baby mementos, wedding gifts…gone.

A friend suggested they could move into this motel, one of many along the road to Walt Disney World. The $179 weekly rate included housekeeping and utilities. Their room at first was just a room, with the king-sized bed hogging most of the space. With just the two of them and the baby, other than not having room for their toddler to move around, they managed. He worked off-and-on, she cared for the baby. About one year into their stay, the relative peace of this arrangement was shattered.

Chris's mother, sister and her two girls lost their place and moved into the same motel. An additional complication – one of the nieces had cerebral palsy and epilepsy. Mom, sis and the girls had a slightly larger room and invited Chris, Carolina and the baby to join them.

Lest anyone think their new room was one of those fairly spacious suites, a two-bedroom, small living room, with a kitchen: wrong. It was the size of an average decent motel room with a half-wall divider creating two imaginary rooms. No kitchen. The dresser held a hot plate and coffee maker. A mini-microwave sat nearby. They requested and received a slightly larger than dorm-sized refrigerator.

They had ever-so-slightly more room than my modest 27' motorhome at the time—a space for one. There were seven of them, including four adults! Bathroom logistics alone created nightmares. Three years of motel hell.

No amount of imagination on my part could perceive the stress. When I asked Carolina, the beleaguered mother, what was the worst part, she spewed a litany of understandable realities. No privacy. No room to move around. Being afraid to wander outside because of drug/prostitution trade using the motel. No neighborly socializing because she didn't know who was in on various nefarious activities. Not being able to have her toddler play in the sand-filled playground because feral cats used it for a litter box. No place to cook a decent meal. An extremely limited menu routine that could be cooked in cramped quarters. Worrying about her toddler reaching up and grabbing the hot plate. Washing dishes in the same place they washed their bodies. Fearing that one of the fairly regular drug raids would turn ugly and inadvertently involve their extended family. This family was there pre-John—the manager when I landed there—when drug traffic and prostitution were rampant. John did a lot to clean it up, but things still weren't good.

Carolina hoped the overwhelmed child welfare authorities would overlook their conditions as they tried to care for themselves.

I asked her what was good. Carolina just as quickly responded. We're together (an understatement!). We aren't on the streets (in a resort town that cares more about their famous mouse than the needs of people). We're able to help our family. The school's wonderful to her sister-in-law's two girls. She gushed about how special the school staff made the girls feel. They had everything they needed to be like the housed-kids. Christmas brought an avalanche of gifts.

Scenes like this play out everywhere, different but the same. I look at motels and think "21st Century Homeless Shelters." I've seen too many to think otherwise.

Storage Units: Need for Stealth

One resounding theme of family homelessness centers around the ubiquitous storage units. The self-storage industry in the U.S. has skyrocketed since the 1960s. Now more than 47,000 storage facilities offer an astounding 1.9 billion square feet of storage space. They give people a place to plop their stuff. Some to never see it again.

Those who've turned to the storage unit solution usually did so when they first became homeless. They'd stash their belongings with great hopes of rescuing the stuff of life when things took a turn for the better. Paying anywhere from $50 a month for a minuscule unit to $200+ for the roomier slots takes a big bite out of limited budgets. People rationalize that it would be cheaper than buying all new stuff. Maybe.

The storage industry has figured out how to lure customers, offering free or low cost first month's rent. The rental agreement specifies how they'll handle arrearages; not with any degree of compassion or reason. Late fees can vary but are quickly boosted to an impossible level.

Indicative of the stress families undergo when they're swirling around in whatever forms of homelessness they are caught, they often fail to pack a "go-bag." The satchel would keep the items of most importance, those hardest to replace. Birth certificates. Insurance policies. Health records. Family photos. The marginally housed need the mental wherewithal to, when the lock-out date approaches, go over and grab the go-bag. Good theory. But stress shreds good theories like tornadoes shred house trailers.

Lost It

On one of my Babes of Wrath trips with Pat LaMarche, we met Lupe, a housekeeper at a chain motel in California. We were finishing our Route 66 tour in 2013. Lupe and her family got booted from their apartment when it was condemned. They had three days to get out. Getting another apartment would have cost an impossible $2,400. They opted for a motel, shoving their stuff in storage.

Lupe had to pay an eye-popping $420 a week for the motel, plus $20 a week for storage. That didn't last long. Her choice was pay the room rent or pay the storage. She described the nice furnishings they had acquired and hoped to keep for their next place. But she got weepy when she described the biggest loss, "All my kids' pictures since they were babies. All their grades. Paperwork. Everything. My baby's blankets that my mom made. We had it all one day. One day we lost it."

Their stuff got auctioned off. Or thrown away.

Stealth Housing 'Option'

Senta, a social worker and mother, fell deeper into homelessness after a disastrous doubled up arrangement shattered. She did what any social worker would do—repeatedly call the local shelter in Wichita, KS to check on openings for her and her 13-year-old daughter. The prospects were bleak. She crafted Plan B.

"I told my daughter, 'it looks like we're going to be living in our storage. We could just say that I'm working at the storage, that's why the bus would have to pick you up there.' I have nowhere else to go. I have a storage [unit]," was her brave take on the situation. "That's going to be our home. It's paid for. We'll have to make it work. I was really scared just because it's cold. But I have a little propane torch and so I told her I'd just burn the propane torch."

At the risk of repeating myself, several parents confessed to considering this a housing "option" when everything fell apart. It's illegal. Evidently, we're good with letting families get so desperate that they consider illegal acts.

Vultures

I was curious what happened when storage facilities held auctions to get rid of stuff that has been confiscated. A few years back, I was in the Atlanta suburbs and saw a sign advertising a storage auction. So I went. Lurking in the back of the crowd, I stealthily took pictures.

It reminded me of the vultures I've seen efficiently tearing apart a carcass. No wasted time. Storage door was opened. Buyers peered in at the mixture of crap and valuable stuff. The "crap" like personal items – like Lupe's kids' pictures and memorabilia – got left behind. The valuable stuff—furnishings, tools, musical instruments, household items—went to the highest bidder. The $38 billion industry knows how to turn a profit. The stuff that used to make a family's house into a home gets scattered to the winds or tossed into the landfill. If I had money and lacked a conscience, I'd buy stock in the storage industry.

Anti-Stuff

My dismazement with the American economy (pre-Covid) included the phenomena of second-hand stores, euphemistically labeled "antique" stores. Yeah, I know some antique stores really sell valuable antiques. But how many of these businesses actually run a profitable operation? And what happens when all that stuff doesn't sell?

When I had to get rid of my stuff, it took a while for me to adjust. Granted, my circumstances forced me to adapt. My new perspective became pretty much anti-stuff. My rule: new thing in, old thing out. Lest I sound virtuous, it's a rule I would like to apply to my digital storage, but I haven't. I need a genie for that task.

True confession: even within the confines of my roughly 120 sq. ft. of living space, I can lose things. That's embarrassing. Annoying. And humbling. Stuff issues are epidemic.

Stealth Stress

More times than I could count, I've stayed where I shouldn't be staying. I'd be desperate for a place to sleep after a long day of driving. If I couldn't find a Camp Walmart to accommodate me, I'd park in a motel or hospital lot. Or I'd discreetly park in a neighborhood.

I've had well-intentioned friends tell me I could stay in front of their house, not knowing that most communities ban people sleeping in vehicles in front of houses. I don't care so much about some obscure regulation, but I've been ticketed (a stern warning, no fine if I moved). I've had an ugly sticker slapped on my window warning of a ticket. Security guards have knocked and made me move, so I know better. Still I do what I have to do. I just try to do it inconspicuously (Ha! A 24' vehicle that looks like a CIA van can't be inconspicuous!).

Maybe it's my Catholic guilt, but when I'm parked in some unauthorized place, I don't sleep well. I dream that someone is pounding on my window ordering me to move. Not too restful. That's the thing about people without homes. They sleep where they can even when they're not allowed or welcomed. They don't sleep well. And not sleeping well leads to a host of other problems.

Lost and Discarded

It's one thing to be lost. But when you are kicked to the curb and don't get any help, that hurts.

Nicole, her husband, their five children—ages 1 - 14, and their dog were evicted in Wisconsin. They had an offer of help from a friend in southwest Michigan, so they crammed everyone in their van and headed across state lines. The offer didn't hold up, a version of the *Grapes of Wrath* I've heard frequently in my travels.

With no money and no options, they slept in their van for a week. "No matter how tired I was, I could not sleep," she told me. "Because it wasn't safe. It was dangerous."

In time they found a small agency to help them. They were connected with an area homeless service provider who put them in a motel for a week. The agency told Nicole that if they found housing during that week, they'd be eligible for HUD housing assistance because they were considered homeless under HUD's definition.

Despite best efforts of the family and the agency, they didn't find any place to rent. Nicole told me that they were turned away from rental opportunities because of bad credit and the size of their family: common barriers. Shelters in that area did not accept intact families. Yeah, consider that—split your family or no shelter. So, they opted to tough it out staying in the motel. They were there two months when I met them in August, 2019.

Nicole astutely articulated what many lawmakers don't get, "The first week that we were in the hotel, it was paid for by emergency shelter services so we were still considered 'homeless.' That gave us a lot more help. But now that we're in the hotel, we live there…" Live there, as not being considered homeless.

To add insult to injury, in order to get housing assistance, she needed to provide birth certificates for her children. Those were lost in the shuffle back in Wisconsin. Getting new documents would cost money and time. So, the family was stuck in that situation until their luck changed. Of course, HUD could change their definition of homelessness to include lost families like this.

Lest we think it is "just" poor people from the ghetto in this predicament, I was chatting with an assistant fire chief in an affluent suburban village west of Chicago a few years back. The economy was still volatile, post 2008-meltdown. He assured me I'd be shocked at the number of area homes in foreclosure with families awaiting eviction. He described the range of sights his crews saw. Some households were all boxed up and ready to go. Others had crap piled around everywhere. The occupants were so depressed, they lost all sense of order. When they hit homelessness, in whatever form, it was undoubtedly a great shock.

Homelessness is Hard to Hide

Hygiene is a huge challenge! Pre-Covid, bathroom access for those without homes was an issue. Many municipalities lock down park restrooms so no one can use them at night. Families sleeping in cars need to get ready for school or work, or just use the restroom during the night.

Too bad for them if the restroom was locked. Some places expend great effort to keep people from cleaning up in public restrooms. I was pleasantly surprised when I was filming in Hawaii to see that, at least back in 2018, restrooms were available, and had showers. Sure, they were spartan facilities, but being able to wash up makes a big difference.

Toilet access fits into this category of hygiene. Most of us have gone into a business or hotel to use a bathroom reserved for paying customers. We got away with it if we looked "normal." Looking normal is hard when you live in places not fit for human habitation. Michigan Nicole described the hygiene challenges for her brood: "Trying to stay clean was a struggle. From being in a vehicle for even a week, when I walk into a gas station, a restaurant or a store to take the kids, we're disheveled. We catch people's attention." So much for stealth.

Parents fear that this attention could lead to unwanted inquiries from child welfare authorities. It's not simply a matter of keeping clean for the sake of human decency. Much more is at stake.

Think of the logistics—especially if one lives in a vehicle, tent, or other unconventional place. Kids go to school in various stages of dirty. It's one of the dead giveaways—teachers notice, classmates notice—and then the "secret" gets out. Dirty bodies and dirty clothes are like flashing lights advertising homelessness.

Every kid I've talked to about school and homelessness says the same thing. They don't want anyone to know their secret—they are homeless. Inevitably, word gets out. If the discovered student is lucky, she/he will get connected with a kind and resourceful homeless liaison. Homeless liaisons are required in every school district across the land. From there, hygiene and other problems can be dealt with. No other students need to know of the homelessness. Teachers are informed on a need-to-know basis. No bullying or shaming should occur. But too often, that's not the reality. Kids can be brutal. So can the adults.

I admit to previously taking showers for granted. My own nomadic shower experiences pale by comparison but they have given me a taste of shower-desperation. I hated the "shower" arrangement in T2, especially after having had a decent little shower in T1. T2's tiny bathroom was converted to a shower room with a curtain. Annoying to mop up afterwards, it also used too much of my limited onboard water. So, I removed the stupid sprayer thing that was supposed to be a shower. I'm now dependent on friends or campgrounds for showers.

Fortunately, I can usually find a shower when I need to be around people. Otherwise I wash up the best I can and deal with it. I've "snuck" into a campground shower on occasion, once getting caught and harshly reprimanded by the camp host. The luxury of having my own shower with my stuff put where I want it to be is now a fantasy. But I'm lucky to get to use some pretty darn nice showers. I tease my friends, rating showers I encounter. I don't think anyone else would care, but I (and I bet my homeless friends) notice all the niceties.

My pride and squeamishness have evaporated. I keep a shower bag with all my essentials, including shower shoes. That was a weird step for me to take, but some showers I've used reinforce my reasoning. A few are horribly gross. A handful of the bathrooms charge to bathe—a quarter for a few minutes of water. Most are presentable. Some are extraordinary! The shower at the Albany, Oregon homeless liaison's office gets a 4-star rating! Decor, accouterments, lighting, space, and more. When I heard a 3-generation family enjoying it, I knew they appreciated the effort that made it a pleasant experience.

The other essential that often is impossible is laundry. Few think of laundry as a luxury. For most of us, it's a dreaded, inevitable task. For those living in homeless situations, even in shelters, doing laundry is like going to a 4-star restaurant. An expensive luxury!

While on my HEAR US 2020 VisionQuest, I stopped to do a load of laundry in a little town in eastern Oregon. Nice new laundromat. But the system required the purchase of a reusable "plastic value card." I was tired. This system flummoxed me so much that the owner, probably watching through their closed-circuit cameras, came out and tried to help me navigate getting the damn card. It required a $10 purchase. My laundry expenses were less than that. He touted that the card would not expire. But I was likely never passing through that way again. How do I get my balance back? Oh. Yeah. That might be a problem. The other problem is many families don't have extra money to sit idly by on a plastic value card that could get lost.

For me it wasn't such a big deal. I handed my card to a beleaguered-looking woman coming in with her load of laundry. But for someone pinching pennies, this would be one of many deal-breakers encountered in the quest for cleanliness.

My friendly liaison in Roseburg, Oregon, toured me around that city a few years ago and showed me their laundromat that opened on certain days/nights to serve those who otherwise couldn't do laundry. For free. Other communities have similar efforts.

Clean clothes and showers go a long way to help a person feel good about themselves. Dignity. Don't underestimate it. If you have to be stealthy about your homelessness, it's nice to not fit the stereotype.

School Bus: Dead Giveaway

When kids are trying to be stealthy about their homelessness, maybe it's because they're staying at a shelter, motel, storage unit or other place that is not a home. They often try to manipulate the school bus driver, asking to be dropped off a block away from their living arrangement. Kind bus drivers figure it out and try to comply.

The humiliation associated with homelessness, especially for kids, is heartbreaking. I've heard countless versions of how kids are ashamed of their situations. Enlightened districts go the extra mile to avoid unnecessary embarrassment for kids—having them picked up first and dropped off last is a common approach. Others arrange for transportation in a van or through a transportation service. Some parents are reimbursed if they drive their kids to school.

Lack of Common Sense

Pre-HEAR US, I met a mom and her freshman son at the high school office in a suburban school district. The vice principal (VP) had previously denied this family the right to attend the school for reasons that typically happen—the administrator didn't know the law about kids experiencing homelessness having the right to go to school. With Project REACH, we had done enough outreach and training that this barrier shouldn't happen, but it did.

Before arriving, I called and spoke with the clueless official. I tried to explain – professionally – the concept was, as I have been known to say after things deteriorate, "… so simple a sixth grader could understand it." After that, I mentioned that I was one of the people responsible for writing the law. *Grrrrr.* I mentioned the student's name and said we'd be coming back to register him as legally entitled to do so.

The family and I met and went into the office. The mother was fine with registering him on her own – after I gave her a crash course in the law. I told her I would hang back and be ready if needed. The office was in the throes of pre-opening registration chaos, filled with parents and students. We waited our turn. I held my breath.

The VP was processing one of the lines of registrants, the one we were in. When the family made it to the counter, he greeted them and shouted out to one of his assistants, "Marge, this is the homeless kid I was telling you about." It was all I could do to not leap across the counter and throttle him. In a busy office, filled with this student's classmates. Great move, Bozo.

I don't recall what got me out of that office without doing bodily harm to him. I do remember the gist of a follow-up call I made, for my sake and for the family's sake. I can't remember a conversation when I really lost my professional demeanor like I did on that call. I did though. I couldn't help it. And I think it helped him grasp the error of his ways.

How Many Others?

A fundamental thing about homelessness? Most people would rather not have others know. It's an understandable stealth thing. Unlike my reasons for stealthy actions, most families experiencing homelessness have plenty of other motivating factors to remain under the radar.

We who think we know this issue, especially when it comes to schools, know that for every student that is identified as homeless under the McKinney-Vento provisions, at least one is not. And that's just school-age kids. Do the math. In 2017-18, schools identified 1.5 million students in various homeless situations. Double that. Then add in more than 1.5 million babies and toddlers who are not counted in the school census. Then add 4 million or so youth outside the system—teens - 25-year-olds. Don't forget their parents.

How can we have millions of kids, with parents and without, who have no place to live? Dismazing.

All adventures, especially into new territory, are scary.

- Sally Ride

CHAPTER 4
Storm Warnings

I'm guilty of not paying adequate attention to weather reports when I travel. At most, I do look at the day's forecast on my iPhone. If something seems troublesome, I might look further—to where I'm headed—and make decisions based on my schedule and other circumstances.

Normally, I head out blissfully, as in "ignorance is bliss," and deal with it. I'm surprised if I remember the reports when I'm ready to get dressed and start moving.

In 2009, as I drove across the backroads of Texas, heading west toward San Angelo, I saw what appeared to be a huge storm cloud on the horizon. *Hmmm,* I remember thinking, *nothing indicated storms ahead.*

I was on a two-lane highway in the middle of nowhere. The thought of turning back didn't occur to me. Changing routes wasn't possible because no roads intersected the one I was on, so I kept going. Wondering. Worrying.

As I got closer, I was even more puzzled, and concerned. That was not a rain cloud. Was it smoke from a fire? I had recently been in an area destroyed by grass fires, and certainly didn't want to be heading toward that kind of disaster. As I got almost to the edge of San Angelo it became perfectly clear what caused this gigantic dark cloud. My path was totally obscured as a dust storm hit with a vengeance. Winds kicked up to a reported 60 mph, making the flying dust a stinging weapon.

My gas gauge was less than a quarter full: the level needed to operate T1's generator when I'm not hooked up to power. I figured that the rapidly dropping temps meant I'd need to run the genny to get heat once I landed in the nearest Walmart lot. I pulled into the gas station at Walmart, put my hooded coat on. I zipped it up so just my eyes peeped out. I had glasses on to provide some protection from the whipping dust. I started pumping. The power went out as I got about $20 worth of gas in the tank. Not great, but it boosted me over the one-quarter mark.

I pulled over to the lot, pointed my rig's nose into the wind, and hung on. When strong winds hit my high-profile vehicle, it rocks like an earthquake. It seemed to go on forever, but it was just minutes. The residue of the storm was visible in my little house. I could write my name in the dust on my table. I had been lucky.

My 'Aunty Em' Story

Kansas has a well-earned reputation for tornadoes. As I was filming *Worn Out Welcome Mat: Kansas* in 2015, I headed out to the western part of the state in T2. I had time, so I stopped in Greenberg, Kansas, where a F-5 rated tornado, the most powerful of these swirling vortexes with winds in excess of 261 mph, had leveled the town in 2007. The locals had built a museum as an educational tribute to the storm that almost wiped them off the map. The rural community was well into the rebuilding process, doing it wisely knowing that another tornado could devastate them. The displays were chilling and brought the reality of tornado damage to us clueless visitors.

My *Wizard of Oz* memory? Back around 1958, my siblings and I gathered in front of our TV to watch this acclaimed movie. The tornado scenes gave me nightmares, as did the Wicked Witch. I've only been near one tornado, as a kid, on a boat with my Dad and siblings. The rough seas had us all leaning over the edge barfing our guts out. And I've seen areas ravaged by tornadoes, so my healthy respect for these storms is well deserved.

My Kansas destination in 2015 was Garden City, in the southwest corner of the state. It was April. The weather was mild. I headed for Camp Walmart on the edge of town, settling in to watch a movie on my laptop. A friend who lives in Kansas and follows my travels texted me that a tornado was headed my way. I looked at a Weather.com map and saw Garden City was right in the path of the storm.

I paused just a moment to decide if I should just stay and press my luck or run like a chicken. The chicken answer won. The storm was traveling directly west to east. I looked at the map for a place in this remote section of the state where I might park. I decided on a blip of a town, Sublette (yet another quirky town name to amuse me). It had a truck stop. Good enough for me. I quickly stowed my loose stuff and took off for the truck stop. It was a muddy parking lot that offered nothing but space to park. I chose a spot next to a big ol' tractor trailer that could act as a wind break. Phew.

The storm didn't hit Garden City, after all. I headed back the next morning and met with the school district's homeless liaison who hadn't run like a chicken at the sound of the tornado warning. She gave me a tour of this small city that reinforced my concept of rural poverty and homelessness. In addition to the impoverished families already there, immigrants and refugees had arrived hoping to survive. They labored at local meat processing plants. Their poverty wages give us our cheap burgers and chicken.

The cloud of poverty in America impacts more than 140 million people. Homelessness is the reality for upward of 10 million, despite the official HUD counts to the contrary. We don't, as a nation, tend to pay any more attention to poverty and homelessness than I do to weather reports. We certainly don't have good poverty-weather reporting mechanisms. And our disaster response efforts leave much to desire.

Disastrous Disaster Responses

I've encountered several major disaster areas in my travels. First, and most mind-blowing, Hurricane Katrina on the Gulf Coast. In 2006, I took a tour of New Orleans' 9th Ward and other parts of the city with my friend Michelle Krupa. Before reporting for the New Orleans Times-Picayune, she was a reporter in Aurora, Illinois and quite interested in homelessness.

The first family I ever interviewed, Melissa N and her family, had been displaced by Hurricane Ivan in 2004 in Florida's Panhandle. That storm's damage was still evident as I drove through the area in January 2006. Melissa's story, which I expand on in Chapter Seven, took me through the saga of a family struggling to survive a major storm, while grappling with the inept response of our nation's disaster response entity: FEMA, the Federal Emergency Management Agency.

I've stared slack-jawed at communities erased by tornadoes. I've witnessed the devastation of fires, both in structures and in the wild. I've seen areas washed away by floods.

I made an unexpected detour in 2019 from my southern I-20 route of my HEAR US 2020 VisionQuest. I headed from the Atlanta area down to the Florida Panhandle at the behest of my friend Katheryn Preston, head of the Georgia Alliance to End Homelessness. I made a contact in Panama City. There, Hurricane Michael, a brutal Category 5 storm (at that time the worst to make landfall) had torn up the Panhandle and even leveled inland Florida and southern Georgia in October 2018.

Kay Daniel, the Bay County School District homeless liaison, welcomed my interest. She knew me from presentations at conferences, so I didn't have to convince her that I was there for the right reasons. Kay introduced me to the stalwart staff working miracles in this vacation community that still laid in rubble 16 months after the storm. Sure, there were some signs of progress for those with abundant resources and good insurance. But a huge swath of the population was either gone (25% by some estimates) or on the slippery-slope journey to recovery.

Employers who managed to work their way back to re-opening had been begging for employees. They hiked wages to above the "generous" $15 per hour mark. Wages like that can tempt people from afar to head to this vacation mecca, much like people were drawn to California's bountiful agricultural industry during the Great Depression.

The big problem here? Property owners have also hiked rents, from $900 for a 2-bedroom unit to more than $2,500. Households struggled to pay rent before Hurricane Michael. After losing jobs, losing housing, and losing assistance, how can the survivors not lose hope? The soaring housing affordability gap means homelessness will batter the vulnerable like hurricane winds.

Before Michael, Bay County school district averaged about 700 students experiencing homelessness. Today they have an unimaginable 3,000. Kay and her staff try gallantly to keep up, but the odds are against them. The trauma of the storm has also impacted her family and most of the school staff. The district has been begging for resources to get more mental health professionals and social workers. Those requests have fallen on deaf ears. I can't begin to comprehend what the Covid-19 crisis has done to the community, and to those like Kay and so many who struggle with their own sanity as they try to give so much to others.

I spoke with Rosie, a self-assured mother of two school-age girls. She described their Hurricane Michael trauma. Huddled in their apartment on the second floor, they kept moving from one spot to another as the walls and roof were torn from their building. They ended up sleeping in an abandoned car, then staying with friends, then moving to Tampa to stay a month in a FEMA-provided motel, and then back to Panama City in a FEMA trailer.

In the process, Rosie pursued a cosmetology license, knowing that she could find work anywhere, especially in an area clamoring for hair professionals. Impressive to be able to pursue such a rigorous course of study while balancing motherhood and homelessness.

When I spoke with her in February, she sounded confident of passing her exams and getting a job before time ran out and FEMA pulled their trailer out from under them in April. That was before the coronavirus upended life in America and beyond.

How Substantial Is Poverty in America?

To get an idea of the vastness of poverty which is the key risk factor of homelessness, consider a few fundamental points that illustrate our nation's abysmal approach to this growing condition.

According to a recent University of Wisconsin – Madison report, "The Census Bureau determines poverty status by using an official poverty measure (OPM) that compares pre-tax cash income against a threshold that is set at three times the cost of a minimum food diet in 1963 and adjusted for family size. The OPM uses calculations of these three elements—income, threshold, and family—to estimate what percentage of the population is poor."

Our nation's way of measuring poverty was changed in 2010, becoming the Supplemental Poverty Measurement (SPM) to factor in 21st Century changes in lifestyle and government policies. It's still supplemental and still not reflective of what grappling with poverty means when you're the one mired in it.

Frustrated by the inadequate way the government measures poverty, the United Way devised another, fairly representative way of determining poverty, nicknamed ALICE. The Asset Limited Income Constrained Employed is a method of quantifying the impact of poverty that reflects realistic household income challenges. It includes those working for less-than-living wages, and it offers a better framework to shape policies and innovative practices.

Even that method comes under criticism. Still, it has generated a sizable amount of attention—among the media and academics—and raised awareness about poverty and wage inadequacies.

The Poor People's Campaign (PPC), a national call for moral revival, picks up where Dr. Martin Luther King Jr. left off. PPC has ignited nationwide activities, marches and political forums to highlight the cost of poverty. They use the SPM, and estimate:

"43.3 percent of the U.S. population — or 140 million people — were poor or low-income in 2017. Our government does not provide information under the SPM on poverty and low-income status for all races, gender identities, or sexual identities. However, according to existing data from the SPM for 2017, the 140 million people who were poor or low-income include:

- 52.1 percent of children under the age of 18 (38.5 million children)
- 40.4 percent of adults between the ages of 18-64 (81 million adults)
- 42.0 percent of our elders over the age of 64 (21.4 million elders)
- 41.6 percent or 65.8 million men
- 45 percent or 74.2 million women

- 33.5 percent of White, non-Hispanic people (65.6 million people)
- 59.7 percent of Black, non-Hispanic people (23.7 million people)
- 64.1 percent of Latinx people (38 million people)
- 40.8 percent of Asian people (8 million people)
- 58.9 percent of Native and Indigenous people (2.14 million people)"

Perhaps not surprisingly, the Trump administration has been exploring ways to reduce poverty by reducing the number of people qualified as poor. Narrowing the definition of poverty, similar to HUD's narrowing the definition of homelessness, reduces nothing except a deceptive statistic.

First Focus for Children, a respected child advocacy group, pointed to the fallacy of this latest squeeze on people in poverty, when representatives stated in congressional testimony, "Modifying the SPM without raising existing thresholds and adopting a consumption measure will only further underestimate child need and downplay the extent of economic instability facing America's families."

Beyond the Theory of Poverty

The theory of poverty is one thing. The reality is another. Let's take a look at the connection between poverty, family homelessness and natural disasters. I interviewed a family in 2012 in Kissimmee, Florida, on the outskirts of Disney World. They could be poster children for families made homeless by storms.

"Pete" and "Jane" illustrate the vulnerability of food service workers. This couple and their young daughter had been fairly secure in their living situation in New Orleans until Hurricane

Katrina hit. Both parents depended primarily on tips. When they lost everything, they fled to Nashville where relatives helped them get back on their feet. Restaurants were plentiful in Music City, and the family returned to their modest version of normal. Five years later, in 2010, massive flooding hit Nashville, again displacing them. The story of what led them to move to Orlando illustrates their beleaguered condition at that point. They turned to their daughter, then eight, and asked her where they should go. She chose the Magic Kingdom. So, they packed up their humble belongings in their aging car and headed south.

They did what countless families do when they lack finances to rent or buy a home—they moved into a motel. Figuring correctly that they'd both get jobs in the shadows of Disney, they planned to be out of the motel world and into a place of their own in no time. The motel was about equally divided between tourists, many from across the Atlantic, and down-on-their-luck families. In fact, the motel and the motel manager reminded me of the Oscar-nominated film, "Florida Project." John, the manager, kept things together in this potentially haphazard operation by keeping his ear to the ground and treating people with respect.

Pete, Jane and their daughter adapted to their new environment. They set their sights on moving out, but the rocky economy of the Great Recession spilled over to the tourist-fueled entertainment industry. Restaurants began cutting back hours, including Pete's and Jane's. Figuring they'd endured plenty of challenges already, they hung tough. But the room cost was breaking them.

They figured out a stop-gap solution. They'd find someone who could split the room cost. They met a man in his 60s, a Navy vet, in the same boat. He had enough to pay for half of the room. Neither parent entered into this unconventional arrangement lightly, knowing that their young daughter needed constant supervision. The family shared one bed, their roommate the other. One parent was always with their daughter.

As they described their situation, they also revealed what is a reality for many income-challenged families. The brakes on their car were shot and they had no money for repairs. They cautiously drove as little as possible, to work and back since public transportation was not an option for their erratic hours.

Having a vehicle is a blessing and a curse. Pete and Jane could barely keep the roof over their heads, so paying hundreds on car repairs was out of the question, even though brakes are safety essentials. Gas was $4 a gallon so every trip was a budget-buster. They saved money for brake pads that a friend agreed to install. Sometime.

Jane had just started a new job at Cracker Barrel. As a new server, she worked two days a week with two tables in her section. Jane was 41 and had been waitressing since she was 17. She needed to hit the ground running with a full schedule.

Jane applied for food stamps but after some delay learned it would be 60 days. In the meantime, they ate breakfast at other hotels that offer complimentary breakfasts. They got some food from a local food bank. She said the schools were really good to their daughter, an honor roll student who easily made friends. Jane stressed that their daughter was never out of their sight when she was not in school. They'd pass her along like a baton in a race—the parent not working, and often not sleeping took over, making sure their daughter's experiences weren't worse than they already had been. Jane shared her anguish when she heard her daughter utter the typical childhood complaints from a kid stuck in these abnormal settings—why can't I have my friends over? Why can't I have my own room? Why can't I go to the places other kids go?

Jane lamented the upcoming Easter holiday. Their daughter, a bright 2nd grader, knew she was in the shadows of Disney World. Her parents would have loved to take her there. They even had a friend who could have gotten them free tickets. But...what kid can go to Disney and not want souvenirs? Or refreshments? So near and yet so far.

Looming in the back of these parents' minds was the reality that they were stuck there. They hung onto a shard of the wreckage of their former life, when they had a home. They survived Katrina, Nashville floods, and then felt the flood waters of a more lethal disaster rising around them. If the government forgot about them— didn't count that they lost housing due to a crisis, didn't acknowledge how precariously they hung on in a tiny, cramped motel room, how they relied on tips and wages from a teetering restaurant economy—they were screwed. No amount of hustle would get them out of that morass.

This family was ineligible for help from HUD because they were not homeless enough thanks to HUD's regulations. They were in a motel, paying for it themselves. Yeah, right. When the bough breaks, the cradle will fall, they will be homeless, child and all. Then they can get help, if they can find it in the land of the shredded safety net.

A Brief, Necessary Detour into the Policy Abyss

Every bit of energy I could spare over the past 15 years has gone to what seems like a hopeless cause—to change the way HUD defines homelessness. My above example of Pete, Jane and their daughter is a classic reason why.

To qualify as homeless, HUD has narrowed the definition in ways that hurt my head just trying to explain it. Briefly, and not the complete picture: if a household or individual lost their housing due to crisis and is staying in a motel on their own dime, HUD doesn't consider them homeless. If they double up (or worse) with family, friends or acquaintances, they're not considered homeless.

In 2007, Illinois Congresswoman Judy Biggert (R-11), now retired, introduced the Homeless Children and Youth Act (HCYA) to align HUD's definition with the US Department of Education's definition (which came straight out of our Illinois Education for Homeless Children Act). We've been fighting for passage of the bipartisan HCYA since then. (To learn more, and to contact your congressional delegation to urge support of this bill, go to www.helphomelesskidsnow.org.)

Sure, it would significantly increase the numbers of kids and adults counted as homeless. Because it should. They are.

The 2020 coronavirus fallout has provided one "benefit." It has called attention to the millions who are doubled up and/or staying in motels because they lost housing and have no resources to get back on their feet. The precarious nature of these arrangements was laid bare as the economy crumbled with the onset of the virus.

Now we really need to address the growing storm of homelessness.

Turmoil Ahead, Prepare to Move

When I interviewed Candace, a 24-year-old mom who had spent four years in the Marines, she recited the doubled-up, car-sleeping, bad-luck, no-hope blues. After falling behind on bills because of an unexpected car repair, she got evicted. "There was a time we were living doubled up, directly across from the apartment we were living in." Candace explained referring to her daughter, "She wanted to go home, and we couldn't." She and her toddler lived out of her car for a while. Then her car was stolen. They bounced around from family members to friends and then to acquaintances.

Her daughter had severe eczema. She scratched as she occupied herself in the Olathe, Kansas shelter's playroom while her mother described the dilemma of being doubled up. During the night, her daughter would scratch and scream in extreme discomfort, waking people up in the household. "It was like walking on eggshells," lamented Candace, "sooner or later they're going to ask you to leave." They did.

The Impact of Living Doubled Up

Each time I interview parents about their house-less condition, I could almost guarantee that they'll mention the same concerns:

- The stressful nature of sharing space not their own, being the visitor who knows they are imposing.
- The fearful sense of knowing they are an argument, or a landlord's visit, away from having to pack up and leave.
- The worries of how this loss of housing impacts their kids, seeing the behavioral changes on a day-to-day basis.
- The frustration of not being able to find a job that will pay enough to move out of the doubled up situation into a home of their own.
- The reality that the lack of childcare means either the host family steps up to watch the kids, or accepting that getting a job is impossible.
- The scant health care system that forces the parent to ignore sicknesses that otherwise would lead to a doctor visit.

- The feeling of "walking on eggshells" where they're staying, or in some cases enduring abusive rants and worse from the host family.
- The hyper-awareness of kids' normal behaviors, keeping such a tight rein on their kids that the children rebel and act out, causing the disturbance that the parent was trying to avoid.

I don't know about you, but I could not last even one night with these worries.

What helps? Knowing that the kids have access to educational stability. Our law (McKinney-Vento Act) removes educational barriers for homeless children and youth. It gives schools clear instructions on their responsibilities to our nation's millions of homeless students. Families in doubled up situations due to hardship are homeless.

Ask almost anyone with company staying at their house for any period of time and you'll hear admissions of frazzled nerves tiring of company. Doubled up isn't housed. Those who are doubled up due to hardship typically have nowhere to go if they are made to leave.

The reality for families—in Orlando, Olathe or anywhere across the country—is that few housing opportunities exist. The common belief that public housing, or subsidized housing, will be there for families could not be further from the truth. Waiting lists are years long. Qualifying for the waiting list is daunting. Evictions, bad credit or past felonies are barriers. The common sense assumption that families can get financial assistance to facilitate their moving into a place is, well, wrong. The slashing of benefits, which were less than meager before the welfare "reforms" of 1996, means that public assistance isn't a factor to help families.

For those lucky enough to get a subsidized housing certificate, finding a landlord willing to accept it is far more difficult than it would seem. The applicant often has to pay a fee, $25 - $50 per adult in the household for background checks, which include credit history. The nonrefundable fee must be paid at each location, resulting in a significant financial burden even before landing a place to live. Unscrupulous property management agencies can rake in the application fees and not rent to the applicants. Credit issues are one barrier.

Furthermore, families must come up with sizable deposits for utilities, and must not have arrearages. Security deposits, with additional charges for pets, are additional barriers. The shortage of affordable housing is a nationwide malady not to be alleviated soon, especially now that the coronavirus has devastated our national, state and local budgets.

Disasters destroy housing. Those with abundant resources and adequate insurance have options to rebuild. The 140 million people who fall in the lowest income categories tend to be renters (at best) and have scant resources or support networks to climb out of any disaster hole. As housing is repaired and restored, those in the middle income levels have a bit more ability to snatch up the limited housing stock. The public or private housing units that had served low-income families are usually the last restored.

What Needs to Change Post-Covid?

The potential for massive housing crises as the 2020 Coronavirus ravages the U.S. economy should frighten all of us. Contingency plans for post-Covid-19 must include adequate steps to address and prevent homelessness, for families and individuals. My wish list includes:

- Change HUD's federal definition of homelessness. Join the campaign I've been involved with for years (www.helphomelesskidsnow.org).
- Offer multiple housing solutions — not one-size-fits-all — for people of all income-challenged levels.
- Accommodate those in the work world who want to escape homelessness.
- Make arrangements in the best interest for kids of all ages.
- Accept that people will stumble and fall, and don't penalize them.
- Make sure every person has access to bathrooms, hygiene, a safe place to rest, health care, nutritional food, mental health services, etc.
- Protect educational access and stability for students of all ages. Consider their needs for tech access, year-round living arrangements, transportation, and childcare, to name a few.
- Build a strong safety net so those on the edge don't fall into homelessness. (Eviction prevention, debt forgiveness, utility assistance, legal help, etc.)
- Establish basic livable levels of income, access to health care, transportation options, quality child care, healthy and affordable nutrition.
- Identify and remove barriers to housing in every community.
- Provide for the elderly and infirm in a humane manner.

Our response to disasters is disastrous! Every time I travel in the Opelousas, Louisiana area, I go by a field where hundreds of empty travel trailers sit, unused, deteriorated and wasted. These FEMA trailers were for households who lost their housing following Katrina in 2005. When I drove by in early 2020, I saw the dilapidated trailers still sitting there.

Fifteen years later.

Dismazed!

We as a nation must ramp up our disaster response. With the frequency of these storms and pandemics we must respond more effectively to keeping people from living on the streets. We certainly have room for improvement. If we don't address the multiple and unending causes of homelessness, we will see it spread like a virus.

The purpose of life is to live it, to taste experience to the utmost, to reach out eagerly and without fear for newer and richer experience.

– Eleanor Roosevelt

CHAPTER 5
No Fair Fare

I was never much of a cook, unlike my siblings. Maybe because I left home right after high school. I wasn't around much during my teen years, popping in for family dinner in between sports, my job and other activities. My siblings all learned their way around the kitchen and they are accomplished cooks thanks to Mom's influence. I was off doing my thing, so I missed these culinary lessons. But her driving skills, and those of my Dad, were thankfully ingrained and have more than come in handy.

As a 16-year-old new driver, I spent as much time behind the wheel as possible. I can remember Mom saying to me, "You'll get tired of driving." No, Mom, on this topic you were wrong. Before she died in 2013 shortly before her 94th birthday, we spoke almost every day, me sharing my adventures and the highlights of my journey. She marveled at my travels, generously supported me financially and offered much encouragement. Dad, who passed away in 2008 at 88, was a consummate driver while he was younger. The wisdom he shared—about driving and grilling— continues to resonate.

My appreciation of good food, which I attribute to Mom, gets satisfied despite my simple regimen. When I land at my sister's, or at culinarily-inclined friends, I totally enjoy what they whip up. I just can't imagine spending the time and effort they spend fixing something that disappears in a matter of moments. I have plenty of excuses for not devoting time and energy to cooking. My tiny kitchen space and lack of storage make it impractical at best. It's good I am totally satisfied with simple, healthy food options.

While running shelters, my meals were often what the volunteers brought for our homeless guests. That took a toll on me, with the almost nightly pasta piling on pounds. Shelter diets are based on what's logistically easy for volunteers to fix and serve. I hate to be critical, but I'd suggest this might not be the healthiest for those staying at shelters.

My imbalanced diet caused a number of health issues. I needed to take control over what I ate and drank. I decided to drop alcohol back in 2002. That was easier when I paid attention to my family tree. My decision was reinforced as I acknowledged the impact alcohol had on many of those staying at our shelter.

I made seismic changes in my food intake back in 1998, following (mostly) the suggestions in *Eat Right 4 Your Type*, the blood type diet, also known as the blood group diet, popularized by a naturopathic physician, Dr. Peter D'Adamo. I dropped about 50 pounds and felt much better.

Living on the road with a small refrigerator, limited storage, and no desire to prepare complicated meals actually worked for me and my health: once I got the hang of it. Both of my mobile homes theoretically made it possible to prepare meals. The issue that the RV designers didn't consider was smell. Fixing a garlic-laden dish would leave me with the smell of stale garlic for days after. It's one thing to smell coffee, but stale food odors do me in.

I opt to keep simple foods on hand: coffee, yogurt, my sister's scrumptious granola, frozen blueberries, apples, manchego cheese, almond butter, gluten-free crackers and bread products, and a few other items, all things that I can stock up on and easily replenish. I carry jugs for drinking water which I refill along the way. I have a small BBQ grill which I'll whip out when staying in a park if I have time. It's a simple, adequate and nutritious approach to food. And I've managed to maintain my weight loss and health, contrary to what many full-time nomads and truck drivers experience.

My friend Pat LaMarche keeps threatening to do a Tillie cookbook with my recipes. Ha! *The Joy of Not Cooking* would have to be the subtitle. I'm not deprived of good food. My simple meals keep me going until I land with my culinarily-inclined connections. And I'll pick up Thai food or eat at Panera or Chipotle on occasion.

Any of us who have food at our fingertips and can make choices about what to eat are privileged. I am. In my thinking, we who have must do what we can to make sure others enjoy adequate nutrition, without red tape, and with dignity. To clarify—I'm not some suffering nomad. I've got modest resources that give me the power to make good food choices. Not so much for the families I've met along the way.

Stuck on a Stick

On one of my longer stints in a Lafayette, LA campground back in 2010, I found myself staring out my camper window on a chilly November day. This campground, a nondescript operation, lacked charm but it was cheap: $12 a night.

One afternoon I spotted an unusual sight—a woman and boy about seven-years-old scrunched down by a campsite faucet. They were washing their clothes and meticulously draping the items on their car to dry. Hmmm. They didn't have a camper or a tent. Hmmm. I looked up from my work and checked their progress as the afternoon went on. They kept at laundry for a long time. Then they made a fire. That got my attention even more. They stuck hot dogs on sticks and roasted them over the fire. No buns. No mustard. No slaw or chips. Just hot dogs on a stick.

This pushed me into motion. Knowing that a nosy woman asking a bunch of questions would be an intrusion, I grabbed an unopened bag of chips and made my way over to my neighbors like the Welcome Wagon lady. They accepted my good-will offering and it opened the door for a brief conversation.

The mom said they went to that campground often because they wanted to get out of the house where they're staying. She didn't use the term "doubled up" but as she spoke it became clear that they were. She said things got tense with her host family, so they tried to not be around much on weekends, except to sleep.

Their hot dog "cookout" cost them the last of their food stamps, which explained the paltry offerings. We chatted about how hard it was to make ends meet, me feeling guilty for my refrigerator of relatively expensive, healthy food. Our conversation was memorable because it was another opportunity to hear from families that are often overlooked. Parents in those dysfunctional situations must "sell" the idea of camping and cookouts as fun. Her son seemed to buy it. In a strange way, these quiet, safe moments become normal respites.

Motel Cuisine

One mom I spent quite a bit of time with in New Jersey back in 2018, Tamu, was bunked up in a tiny motel room with her six-year-old daughter, and three sons, 10, 16, and 21. Their room offered no privacy or cooking facilities, just a microwave and dorm-size refrigerator.

We hit it off nicely. They understood and were excited about the purpose of the film I was making for the New Jersey Department of Education's McKinney-Vento Homeless Education department. They welcomed the opportunity to share with me on camera.

I hung out there on a Saturday since Tamu didn't work weekends and the kids were around. I tried to be like a fly on the wall, capturing life as it happened inside the dismal 15' x 15' space. I lurked in the parking lot when the kids went out to play amid the trucks and cars that ruled this dingy "neighborhood."

Tamu worked full-time at a nonprofit organization that appreciated her skills and paid her a decent wage. Her job made it possible for her to keep her family off the streets.

That area of west-central NJ has few shelters, and none where her family would be able to stay intact. The way many shelters work: her two older boys would have to be separated from her and the younger ones. A deal breaker for Tamu. The motel "choice," which many families can't afford, costs upward of $250 a week. She spent all her modest wages on food and motels.

Amassing $2,000 or more to move into an apartment, which seems like a logical approach, was impossible. Renters must fork out hundreds for utility deposits and have $50 or so for application fees just to be considered as a possible tenant. The motel route is, for some, the simplest. But it's grueling.

The biggest issues families face in these small spaces is the lack of privacy. Anyone who has stayed in a motel should be able to imagine that. Pack in 4 or more people, as Tamu and so many families do, and you've got an emotional tinderbox. Tensions can flare with barely a spark. The close quarters also mean that if one gets sick, they all get sick. Storage is a nightmare requiring organizing skills and rigid enforcement. Doing schoolwork on the bed, with the TV blaring and siblings distracting, does nothing for academic achievement.

Tamu didn't have a car, and public transportation is almost nonexistent in this area, as with most other places I filmed. "Grocery shopping" typically consisted of her older kids going over to the truck stop convenience store across from the motel. They purchased the kind of food that didn't require cooking. They whipped up sandwiches with cold cuts, chips, and a jug of orange drink. I cringed as I filmed the process, knowing that the intake of processed foods did nothing but assuage their immediate hunger while deteriorating their health.

"My children, they're used to eating. I was a wife and mother that cooked every day," Tamu lamented. Twenty years of marriage didn't prepare her for this wabi-sabi existence, but she had no choice. After her divorce, she and her kids bounced from family member to family member as long as they could. Doubling up, they tried to carve out a new normal after leaving their three bedroom house with a fenced-in yard. She recognized the doubling up hazards, sagely observing, "There's only room for one cook in the kitchen."

Every mother I spoke with along my travels shared similar regrets—most often describing in painful detail – memories of their holiday meals, filled with food and family. Among so many other things, homelessness causes a massive erosion of lifestyles. Kids adapt. Parents yearn.

Lunch-Shaming Poster Child

One food-related issue I've encountered and become more involved in is lunch-shaming: the practice of some schools that penalize students when their school lunch accounts are in arrears. The more flagrant response to this ridiculous issue is throwing the student's lunch tray, filled in error with food, into the trash, in front of the student body assembled to eat. I've read horror stories of how schools punish kids for owing lunch money. We should be ashamed of lunch-shaming.

"Tuna-Gate," the Cherry Hill, New Jersey effort to shame poor families into eking out lunch money or get served a tuna sandwich, caught the attention of our alter ego twosome, "Babes of Wrath," in September 2019. It worked out that Pat LaMarche and I, aka Babes of Wrath, were available to head to Cherry Hill. We wanted to investigate the school district's problem collecting lunch money from families too poor to pay. We met with the district's homeless liaison. She confirmed our concerns that they might be missing some kids who'd otherwise qualify for free lunch because they are homeless. Students experiencing homelessness are automatically eligible for free lunch without paperwork.

In pre-coronavirus days, we seemed to have a national lunch-shaming epidemic, districts putting the squeeze on families to force payment for school lunches. Babes of Wrath, with our decades of work with impoverished and homeless families, believe that school districts may be lashing out when they should be looking out for families, those with housing and without, who cannot afford lunches.

It's common that districts don't recognize students experiencing homelessness. Families often don't self-identify, for shame or fear of child protective services getting involved. Or they just think they're "going through hard times," and try to cope, falling behind on payments they may not even need to be making because they qualify as homeless. Since Cherry Hill doesn't have a shelter, many families double up, stay in motels or sleep in vehicles.

"With vast economic disparities, families are doing the best they can to survive and make sure their kids get an education. School lunch shouldn't be the stumbling block," asserted LaMarche. Her years of running shelters in the Carlisle, Pennsylvania area taught her that often kids go to school hungry. Being deprived of school meals only worsens their school performance.

Based on work I did for the New Jersey State Board of Education, it was my contention that this district had a math problem. Although Cherry Hill has a poverty rate of only three percent, they have about 1,500 students receiving free lunch, representing very low-income households. The district has in the past identified about 50 homeless students over the course of the school year. In fact, according to modest estimates, 10% of the free-lunch recipients are homeless. Under-identifying keeps students from getting the help they need to succeed in school. The district should have identified at least 150 students as homeless.

"Who performs well when they're hungry?" was my question to the school district's homeless liaison when we met with her. Erecting barriers to food and shaming kids is senseless. Babes of Wrath challenged the Cherry Hill School District to decide on a policy that doesn't involve plunking a tell-tale tuna sandwich on a lunch scofflaw's tray. In the end, they decided to limit punishment to those students about to graduate, not letting them walk the stage on graduation night. Right. A kid fights poverty and homelessness and still manages to graduate, and they want to deprive the student of the honor of the graduation ceremony? That stinks.

What added to the stink was when we headed over to the local food pantry and spoke with several families waiting to get groceries. They must meet stringent income requirements to qualify for food assistance. Every adult we spoke with, many of them grandparents, indicated that they had family members, including school-age kids, doubled up with them because they families lost housing due to crisis.

That's a classic element in the McKinney-Vento education definition of homelessness—lost housing due to hardships, moving in with someone because you have nowhere to go. We asked if they had received information from the schools about free lunch. No.

Did the schools know they had people doubled up, aka homeless? Yes.

A quintessential gap. It takes constant, relentless outreach to get the word out about the "benefits" of the McKinney-Vento provisions, which include free lunch, without filling out a bunch of paperwork, to students who qualify as homeless. Evidently the school district dropped the ball. We left flyers at the food pantry. The Philadelphia Inquirer covered our visit, which hopefully caught the attention of Cherry Hill school officials. Beware the Babes of Wrath.

Now, "thanks" to the coronavirus, we don't hear about lunch-shaming. Instead, kids and families are highly mobile, thereby missing the food assistance efforts being carried out by school and community volunteers. Who would think we'd miss the good ol' days of lunch-shaming?

Babes Feast

While on the topic of food, and the Babes of Wrath, my mind wanders back to our 2013 Rt. 66 tour. Pat and I were heading west out of Albuquerque and it was getting late. We found a no-hook-up, free Bureau of Land Management campground that offered a breathtaking view of the landscape.

We whipped out the BBQ grill, and slow-cooked turkey legs. It's hard to be patient when you're hungry, and we were, but we knew the final product would be worth it. My Dad used to mix sugar and oil, drizzling it over the chicken or turkey on the grill. Easy technique, and simple ingredients (1/3 sugar, 2/3 oil).

If you ask either of us what our most memorable meal was, this was it. We stood, gnawing on these meaty, crispy, sweet legs, looking at the sunset over the stark New Mexico desert. Hard to explain to most people, but this was a huge perk of HEAR US travel. Nice to have someone to share it with! Pat always enjoys her Babes travel with me. And I love having her contrarian self to travel with.

Motel Meal Speed Bumps

A few years back, I was advocating for a family stuck in a motel, trying to track down resources before I sent them on a wild goose chase. I called the local food pantry to inquire about requirements and hours.

Their representative told me they don't serve "motel families." *No?* They believed these families were transient. This was long after the "trend" of families turning to motels because no shelters operated in their communities. It's a continuing, inexcusable trend that affects many people. Memo to those running food assistance programs that exclude motel families: hunger hurts.

I get the concept of not being able to serve everyone because your supplies are limited. I ran a shelter with limited space. We needed to set guidelines because of the very real dilemma of severe overcrowding with local people needing help. Our community was on a train line connected directly to Chicago. And we had a handful of folks with no ties to the area who heard a news story about our nice suburban shelter and decided to come out. I don't blame them. I'd try too. We set the most humane guideline we could, a night of hospitality and then offer help getting back to Chicago or wherever they had a place to stay. That was horribly painful for staff. Not to mention to the person who had hopes of a better opportunity in a new community.

This food pantry had no such wiggle room. No motel families. Period.

Think of the logistics of acquiring food, storing it, cooking it, serving it and cleaning up your dishes in a motel.

I've been in motels where the bathtub served as the refrigerator. Nice, until someone needs to bathe. Crockpots are helpful, but often forbidden. The smell of a spicy pot of chili wafting down the motel hallway might be a bit off-putting. Ditto for hotplates. I guess the latest fad of instant pots, an appliance beyond my experience, is a no-no in motels, too.

Ramp Up the Fight Against Hunger

Getting food is an obstacle, especially for the income-challenged. Food stamps, aka SNAP (Supplemental Nutrition Assistance Program) card benefits, have been slashed to the point of ridiculous. The feds don't think families in homeless situations need as much food assistance as non-homeless households. What the well-fed bureaucrats haven't figured—it's hard to stretch food resources when you have to buy processed food requiring no refrigeration and minimal preparation. Special dietary needs get ignored. Infants get what they get. Formula gets watered down. Nutrition be damned. Health issues skyrocket because of our refusal to make nutritious food available.

Weekends, holiday breaks, summer, and now the coronavirus "holiday" snaps the food chain that schools offer. Gallant efforts to feed families-in-need are being ramped up. But now we're realizing how many actually need food assistance. A lot.

SNAP benefits, meager as they are, make an easy target for any administration wanting to punish people for being poor. The 2020 legislative session is no exception. Congress has tossed around possible restrictions on who qualifies for food assistance, how to balance the budget by slashing food assistance, ways to cut school lunch programs, and reducing nutritional standards of school lunches. Compassionate, knowledgeable lawmakers are fighting against the slash-and-burn contingent. Why don't more legislators realize that kids are people, too?

At the same time, the coronavirus crisis has pushed the U.S. Department of Agriculture to explore ways to make it easier to get food to families that had previously relied on school lunches. One effort would be to give families money in place of free/reduced lunch benefits. CNN reported this provision, the Pandemic EBT (P-EBT, Electric Benefit Transfer), would come to about $114 a month per child. This would be enormously helpful, but the logistics seem to be daunting. Families will get missed. Hungry kids. Hungry adults.

Unfortunately, the wheels of government move at a snail's pace when it comes to helping those who need help the most. Billions were dispersed in "small business" assistance in a heartbeat, although the definition of "small business" got seriously distorted along the way. Not so fast for the paltry food assistance, P-EBT. Six weeks after the legislation was approved, only four states had been granted permission to put this program into effect. It's time-limited. It was supposed to end as the federal fiscal year ends, in September. Knowing how disasters take a lot longer to remediate than anyone would think, it's extremely likely that this assistance would be needed long after September. It would be nice if every state could ramp this up and get food money into the hands of hungry families. Nice, but I'm not holding my breath.

How quickly can most of us underestimate, or diminish, the need for adequate nutrition, especially for babies, toddlers and children in their critical developmental period? Tossing a few granola bars their way hardly makes a dent. We tolerate, by omission, massive slashes to food assistance programs. I say this by way of confession.

That's one reason I've decided to take on the issue of lunch-shaming, to focus my energy, my bully pulpit (long on bully, short on pulpit) to fight for food for those who need it and can't get it. And though, like I said, this coronavirus shutdown has eliminated lunch-shaming, it will be back with a vengeance once schools return to face-to-face learning.

Fight Over Food in the Fridge

Doubled up is the common temporary housing status for a big chunk of families (about 75%) experiencing homelessness. Few policymakers realize how difficult it is to maintain equilibrium in an overcrowded household where at least some of the occupants are stressed to the max. The reality, guests—usually with kids in tow—become an imposition, and a disaster-in-the-making in a short time. Just think back to any time you've had company stay for too long.

Families in that doubled up cycle are at the mercy of their host family. They're in a crisis mode, traumatized to some degree, income-challenged, and fearful that their situation will crumble before they get settled. They seldom unpack the garbage bags filled with their belongings.

Leia and her kids in Texas bounced around like tumbleweeds after they were evicted. When I met up with her in 2013, they had just moved into yet another temporary housing arrangement. She told me about a previous situation where "I had just spent about $400 on groceries. I think something made the host family upset…we ended up having to leave and left $400 worth of groceries there because I wasn't able to take them [the groceries] with us."

I've heard doubled up tales of woe including kids eating their host family's food by mistake, causing an uproar. Sometimes the host family eats what their visitors bought, causing hard feelings. Or the host family doesn't invite their visitors to eat with them. Judgmental statements are flung at the visiting parents about needing to get a job before the hosts will share food.

Food may seem like a little thing, but these little things cause the biggest blow-ups.

Food, Food Everywhere

I haven't experienced true hunger, probably ever. I've barely missed meals. I travel with a refrigerator, freezer and microwave filled with food of my choosing. I shop in stores that have an obscene array of choices. I can eat when I want, what I want. That makes me privileged. With privileges come responsibilities.

For me, I've tried to develop a sense of gratitude for all who made it possible for me to enjoy whatever food is before me. I've realized more than ever that food workers—those harvesting, packing, transporting, selling food—are the most under-appreciated people in our country. That is another reality that has emerged from the Covid crisis. Too bad it takes a crisis to realize the good that we have.

My awareness of food servers includes those who leave work and head to homelessness or are fighting to avoid losing their humble abode. That pushes me to tip. Generously. Because I can.

The plethora of issues surrounding food—who raises and processes it, who transports it, who sells it, who cooks it, who cleans up after we eat—deserve our awareness, and our action. I've driven by countless fields where workers do the backbreaking labor to get the food to clueless consumers. These workers live in third-world conditions, and are paid paltry sums. They lack access to health care or even basic hygiene. Some fear the call to Border Patrol and deportation—they are often the ones making sure we have fresh fruits, vegetables, and meat. I need to ramp up my fight for justice for those who get our food to us.

Food access and housing, or lack thereof, are critical concerns, not just for those struggling with access to those basics, but for all of us. I want the person preparing, serving and cleaning up after my restaurant meal to be healthy and happy. Same for those, many of whom are migrants, who do the backbreaking work to get our food to us. It's common sense.

Nutrition for my Mind

As someone who spends long hours driving, I have choices. Where and what I eat. That goes for what I feed my brain, too. When I first started this trek, I made a decision. Listen to music, not news or talk radio or anything else that would cause me to overdose on anxiety.

I ingest a measured, deliberate dose of news in the morning on my iPad. I peruse the stories about family/youth homelessness and poverty, posting on Facebook in my "Diane Downer" mode. From there I scan the New York Times, CNN, Guardian and assorted feeds to see what's going on in the bigger world. Then I can settle into mental exercise—the NYT crossword—to accompany my breakfast. After that, I'm ready to go.

Music has saved me. My Spotify feed can keep me happily rolling for hours. Among my favorite performers: Carrie Newcomer and Sara Thomsen. But I have an eclectic selection of everything from folk, pop, classical to undefined. When music surrounds me; I can think. It massages my brain. I joke about being one of the few people in the country with the luxury of time to think. That's probably not a joke.

As I listen to stories of families enduring unimaginable hardships and struggling with health issues, I agonize over the inequity of life here in America. Some of us can take extraordinary measures to stay healthy. Millions lack even the basics of nutrition to get through the day. Many work harder than I could ever work. "No fair!" doesn't begin to describe this injustice.

Start where you are.
Use what you have.
Do what you can.

- Arthur Ashe

CHAPTER 6
Road Hazards

Warning signs everywhere. Caution, one-lane road. Caution, free-range grazing. Caution, falling rocks. Caution, construction ahead.

The One-Lane Squeeze

My first year of travel, my enormous RV, Tillie1, and I were heading east through Pennsylvania. It was 2006. I had just finished a grueling set of interviews of kids in Lancaster. I mentally processed those encounters as I drove east to my next filming stop in Virginia. Somehow, I ended up on a backroad that seemed like it was going in the right direction. I couldn't be sure. My GPS was no help because I lacked a signal.

May brings nice weather and road construction. I was on a skinny two-lane road when stopped by a flagger. The woman stood next to her little red wagon loaded with a cooler and water bottle. I was first in line when she waved us through the one-lane opening. As I slowly started moving, her wagon rolled into my path. I edged over to the right alongside the rocky hill to try to avoid crushing it.

In the process, I scraped the rocky face of the hill on the right side of my rig. I heard a dreadful grinding noise as I tore up my step and popped my right rear tire. Nothing prepared me for this encounter. I hopped out, knowing I was blocking traffic. I took a quick look at the obvious damage (grateful for dual rear tires), glared at the flagger who had by then corralled her wagon, and hopped back to drive to a nearby safe spot and regroup.

Amazingly, I was able to get a cell signal and called road service. They sent someone out who changed the tire, but he wasn't able to address the structural issues. The bent metal from the scrape remained. I could tell the damages were extensive, so I called my insurance agency and they sent a wrecker. As the tow truck driver drove my poor lame rig onto the bed of the truck, the newly-replaced tire was punctured by the bent metal.

Seeing my 10'4" high vehicle on the flatbed of the truck gave me further reason to worry as low-hanging branches combined with the height of the truck and my vehicle could mean further disaster.

Fortunately, we made it to the repair shop without further encounters of the worst kind. The logistics of the repair meant I needed a hotel room and rental car. Budget-busting expenses. I never imagined that the repairs would be finished the next day, but they were. Happily, my insurance covered most of it, though the deductible left me quite broke. I gingerly made my way out of town a day late, more than a dollar short.

Pass Fail

Oregon, 2011, also provided some backroads adventures of the worst kind. Following a session filming a mom and baby living in their car in a beach town, I naively made my way down the spectacular Oregon coast. It was May, and things couldn't have been prettier, so I stayed on the coastal highway longer than I should.

Checking the atlas, I saw Bear Pass, one way to get to Medford, my next destination. That gave me max ocean drive, and minimum interstate. Great. Naive. Many mountain passes don't open up until summer. As I ventured across the rough gravel road that would take me to Bear Pass, I learned two valuable lessons. Some gravel roads are not fit for driving on with a rig such as Tillie.

And just because the atlas says a road goes through, doesn't mean they won't close the pass. Which is what happened.

Having driven on mostly one-lane, hellish-gravel roads for miles to get to the closed pass sign, I had a decision to make. Turn around and go back—a bone-jarring ride on a road that I just came from (and swore I'd never travel again) or proceed to what seemed to be an alternative, hopefully viable route. I took Plan B, and found myself going through the minuscule town of Agness, where a small group of locals gave me that *dumb tourist driving an RV down a horrible gravel road* look. I was praying to my deceased Aunt Agnes by this time because these roads were still as bad as the ones I had been on thus far.

A sign said 10 miles of gravel roads. While that doesn't sound so daunting, I will never forget the sense of doom I felt while slowly inching my increasingly rattling Tillie1 toward paved roads again. When I finally got to solid ground, I wanted to get out, kneel down and kiss the road. Instead, I pulled over and assessed the inside damage. My pull-out, the motorized extension that expands the living area where I sat and worked, had sustained significant damage. The rough roads had caused my heavy file cabinet to bounce like a basketball on that pull-out platform. I could tell by looking at the askew platform that it was toast. I didn't even look at the outside of my rig. I figured I'd hear the rattles if something was broken.

This was one of those "damned if you do, damned if you don't" situations. I don't know the best thing I could have done. I did develop a deep respect for mountain passes. I mentally kicked myself for getting into that mess. Errors in judgment—however unintentional—cost money and are dangerous. I was lucky.

Snow Kidding

A post-script: a few days later, on Mother's Day, having finished my filming in Medford, I decided to venture up to Crater Lake. That spectacular national park in Oregon has a deep lake so blue and beautiful. When I left the lowland park, it was sunny and in the 60s.

I started getting a clue about weather changes when I saw spots of snow in the woods that increased in depth and dimension as I got closer to the park. During my cursory glance at the atlas, I failed to notice Crater Lake was on the top of a mountain. The roads were clear and traffic was light, so I persevered, determined (the word that should be the red flag for me!) to see this natural wonder.

The snow got deeper than any I've ever seen. I pulled over and climbed onto my rig's ladder all the way to T1's 10-foot high rooftop. I took a picture that showed the snow alongside the road was as high as the top of Tillie. I kept pushing on. Fortunately, the roads were clear!

I paid to get into the park. By that point I felt like I might have made a mistake. When I got to the park's central business district, it snowed like crazy. The freestanding port-a-potties had 6 feet or more of snow on the top! *Guess I won't be camping here tonight* I thought as I carefully made my way out of the park.

Signs with a Purpose

Naturally, with all the backroads I've traveled, I have no end of tales of woe that involve road hazards. At first, I was nonchalant as I crossed a Nevada desert with signs warning about grazing animals on the loose. Suddenly, I would confront free range critters blocking my path in the middle of nowhere. California highway signs warned of falling rocks. I didn't take that too seriously until I came around the corner and screeched to a halt to avoid crashing into a humongous boulder that just landed right in the middle of my lane.

On the other hand, "curve ahead" signs with a lower speed limit mean slow down. But I learned my rig could safely handle being 10 mph over the posted level. If things were clear. Early on I detected impatient drivers behind me if I drove the slower speed limit. Pushing the limit, in my thinking, kept me safer.

While we have abundant road signs advising us of how to safely navigate a vehicle, that doesn't happen in life. Mothers often don't see the danger down the road of relationships. When they perceive a warning sign, it is often too late. They're down the road without a roadside assistance policy.

Warning Signs Needed and Heeded

In the barely-a-town of American Falls, Idaho in October 2019, I interviewed three mothers (Keri, Teri, Christina), each with three children. First, grasp the fact that these three families were only the tip of the iceberg of families experiencing homelessness in this town of just over 4,000. Since the start of classes that year, the school district's homeless liaison, in a district with 1,400 students, had identified at least 105 students experiencing homelessness. That didn't include babies and toddlers in their families, or older teens. That's up from 55 the previous year, and was pre-pandemic.

Now, wrap your mind around the reality that if not for the tenuous temporary housing arrangements each of them had with family members, being doubled up, they would have nowhere to go. The closest shelter, in Pocatello, was almost an hour away and runs at full capacity.

Each of these mothers saw the danger signs in their relationships. Keri observed, "We'd been together for 15 years and he just started changing…" Teri pointed to the signs she saw, "There was a lot of emotional, physical, sexual abuse going on…" And Christina simply stated, "After a falling out with my relationship…" The bottom line, these 3 moms had to scramble to find a safe place to live. They each voiced deep concern about the shaky nature of their current housing, and admitted they had nowhere to go if these frazzled arrangements fell through.

Drivers' Education, Relationship Education

For many reasons, the warnings of domestic violence often go unheeded until too late. All these moms recognized that they had no options. Their incomes were not even close to being enough to make it on their own. Child support? Too frequently that's a theory. The reality is many fathers don't pay. The pattern of leaving and returning to the abuser is complicated, but it often has roots in the economic uncertainty the mother and kids experience.

When you think of what it takes to live independently, especially with children, the great majority of families in the middle to lowest income levels face tough choices if they need to leave a relationship. Scarce domestic violence shelters typically are at or are over capacity. Many areas, especially rural ones like American Falls, have no services for families in domestic violence situations, or those experiencing homelessness, for that matter.

Survival takes money. It takes credit cards, bank accounts, mailing addresses, and all the day-to-day things we take for granted. One of the mothers I interviewed in American Falls, Keri, said she didn't have a car or cell phone. She had to rely on a frayed connection with her sister to escape her abuser.

Domestic violence is a primary reason families become homeless. Our disregard of the value of families, failing to provide them the support they need to survive, is a warning sign we must heed. If families don't matter to society, what road do they end up traveling? What training do young people get for the challenge of navigating a relationship and family? How many couples end up together but without any clue as to what relationships require? A quality course in relationship education, comparable to drivers' education, would be worth considering.

Identified the Hazard: Cluelessness

From the first days of HEAR US, I've been involved in a grassroots movement to change the way HUD defines homelessness. I have ranted about this issue in several places in this book, starting with Chapter 3. Why is this such a big deal, you wonder?

The definition debate is at the heart of family homelessness. HUD's definition excludes at least 80% of families experiencing homelessness, removing any possibility of assistance to escape homelessness. Worse, HUD's woefully inaccurate assessment of homelessness aids, abets and validates the paltry annual sum Congress appropriates for homelessness. The Homeless Assistance Grant hovers around $2.5 billion. Since HUD's definition fails to include millions of families, youth and non-chronic adults, Congress thinks HUD has the situation under control. That couldn't be further from the cruel truth.

What I fail to understand is why. Why do some so-called homelessness advocates lead the charge for HUD's distorted ways? I've been at this advocacy a long time. I've identified a few people and motivations that appear responsible for these policies.

Leading the charge for HUD over the past decades has been the National Alliance to End Homelessness (NAEH). They provide technical assistance to HUD. Nan Roman, NAEH head, has been an ardent foe of expanding HUD's definition. Our paths have crossed a few times, one being our 2007 testimony to the House Ways and Means subcommittee that oversees HUD.

By that time, I had traveled enough and talked to enough people to know that those in the trenches by and large found the HUD definition and the 10-Year-Plan to End Homelessness a bunch of hooey. I gave my testimony, Nan gave hers. She extolled HUD's efforts stating, "The HUD McKinney-Vento programs have been well-run over the past 20 years, well-administered by HUD, and well-delivered by a network of nonprofit and faith based providers..." She continued, saying the shelter system shouldn't be expanded, that efforts to end homelessness shouldn't be focused on one population or the other: children or adults. Sure, she stated that families need to get back into housing faster. But broadening the definition of homelessness, "is a bad idea."

Her reasoning, "it would mean 3.8 million more people would be eligible for assistance..." requiring a cool $7.8 billion to address their needs. And she declared those doubled up for economic reasons are not homeless.

I'll just say a few things. How can you recognize the significant number of vulnerable housing-impaired households and not push for them to get help if you are the head of the national organization dedicated to ending homelessness? How can you say HUD's doing such a wonderful job when homelessness is soaring— as it was then and continues to be?

I suppose if I were in her position, and my main funder was HUD, I'd probably spew the same BS. But I'm not. And I won't. And I can point out the pattern of deception on how HUD is creating homelessness, not ending it. I've seen and heard from people in the system and those irreparably harmed by extended periods of homelessness—adults, families and youth. I've been involved with advocacy to strengthen HUD's approach to homelessness for decades. HUD, despite whatever best efforts of individuals, is not well-run or well-administered. Nor are their services well-delivered. If they were, we'd see a genuine approach to address homelessness for all categories of people, including families.

The Covid crisis of 2020 has illustrated the scope of homelessness like nothing else. Obviously, those on the streets needed to be isolated so they weren't getting infected and infecting others. Families stuck in motels with nowhere to go needed support to maintain their temporary accommodations. Those doubled up needed support to stay where they were or to find an alternative arrangement. Providing temporary housing—often motels/hotels—strained communities trying to reduce the infection rate. Shelters have struggled too, but the bulk of the homeless population is outside the shelter system. They're the ones that have caused some officials to finally get a clue on how many people in this country have nowhere to live.

Perhaps I'm being kind calling Nan and her believers clueless. Maybe a better word would be callous.

Trauma, Abuse

The resilience of parents and kids in abusive situations continues to amaze me. The pervasiveness of trauma-inducing abuse dismazes me. Sexual abuse is one common form of trauma I've encountered among the families and youth I've met. Trauma, in its many shapes, shatters a person's self-esteem, and can cause physical and mental health issues into adulthood.

Sexual abuse is a horribly difficult subject to raise, for me or for those listening to or reading my observations. I'm not a medical or mental health professional. What I know comes from what I've read and what I've heard from countless kids and parents. Those experiences were devastating, and created problems that cause chronic suffering in all sorts of ways. People who have been abused often try to build a secret wall around their experiences. Understandable, but when not publicly discussed, each victim feels like they're the only one. Silence further ravages those abused.

Early in my travels I met a family desperate to escape homelessness. The family had been doubled up with a family member. That had shattered into pieces of pain and betrayal. The Las Cruces, New Mexico school district bent the rules to place the family in a local motel while they worked with the mother on options.

The district's homeless liaison came up empty-handed. She desperately turned to me, hoping I could interview the mom and perform a miracle. I had no solution in mind but wanted to meet this 22-year-old mother and her children. They asked the young woman's permission and she agreed. I made it clear that I had no answers or miracles. Her story might, if nothing else, help other families in similar situations.

Tina, pregnant with her rapist's baby, had five little boys all aged ten and younger. They huddled on the double bed in a darkened, nondescript Las Cruces motel room. By noon they would be out on the streets. She had a last-ditch plan. A friend loaned her 13-foot camper, already waiting for her in a hardscrabble RV park. She and her boys could camp until she could get something else worked out. I shuddered at what I knew would be incredible hardships for this family.

In the six months she and her boys spent in that little tin can camper, they endured frigid cold and scorching heat. Unimaginable chaos was inevitable with all those bodies in such a confined space.

I can't fathom what Tina went through in those last six months of her pregnancy. The discomfort as she neared her due date had to be grueling. Taking care of her boys would have been hard enough. She had the three littlest ones all day. The bus came and transported her two oldest boys to their schools. To their credit, they didn't miss a day.

Advocates searched for options. The standard solution—get the family into subsidized housing—proved impossible. Tina and her soon-to-be ex-husband owed $3,000 to the housing authority in Arizona. After she left him to escape his abuse, he managed to stay in the apartment rent-free for months. Both names were on the lease so she was responsible for half.

In 2009, the federal government instituted a short-lived housing effort, HPRP (Homeless Prevention and Rapid Rehousing Program). This one-time $2 billion fund was a way out of the camper for Tina and her family. But it was temporary, and to qualify for a regular housing certificate (Section 8), her debts needed to be paid.

Eventually, after plenty of resource wrangling, Tina and her children, including her new baby boy, moved into a Section 8 house. She couldn't work because childcare was impossible to find, much less afford. The inadequate government assistance she received—medical care for her children and food stamps—helped. The cash shortfall was daunting. The fathers of her children paid child support sporadically. She and her mother were estranged, so that avenue for support was closed.

The tangible challenges Tina faced were formidable. The dark cloud of trauma was even more devastating. From early on she had been sexually abused. She had no family support. Her succession of relationships with abusive men reflected her devastated self-worth.

The family cascaded through a series of subsidized housing units. These frequent moves were caused by landlords and the housing authority. They often deemed her housing placement unfit, because of dangerous drug activity nearby or heavy infestation of bugs. Nonetheless, Tina's household was orderly and functioning. Despite battling the creepy-crawlers, criminal activities of neighbors, abject poverty, deep depression, and more, Tina kept things together.

The few helpers she had on her side saw her strengths. None of us imagined her escaping the shackles of deep poverty and homelessness. I was involved with her in a limited way over these years. Normally optimistic, I had a hard time imagining how she and her children would ever move beyond their dire circumstances. I would visit her and her kids whenever I went through Las Cruces and we would email or talk once in a while.

I had to overcome my own prejudices. I'd see Facebook posts of Tina out with friends and I'd bristle at what I read into these encounters. The pregnancy thing—we don't think women should get pregnant if they don't have the resources to take care of their babies—always eats at me. From previous experiences at our shelter, I knew women who struggled to avoid getting pregnant. They often lacked of birth control or were sexually abused. My white, middle-class, non-parent way of thinking struggled to understand the complicated reasons women end up pregnant. I knew I needed to adjust my narrow thinking about women who become pregnant.

I'd see her Facebook posts describing social gatherings. I worried about her choices in significant others. Men who, according to her descriptions and their Facebook profiles, seemed to have nothing in mind but partying. I'd read her account of fights with these guys, and follow her emotional turmoil with a sense of dread. The patterns were predictable—meet someone, date a few times, discover the flaws in the relationship. The break-ups were brutal. I could feel her depression from thousands of miles away.

From what Tina had shared with me, I knew she had very little guidance in relationships. The trauma from her abuse followed her like a tumbleweed caught under the axle. She couldn't shake it off, and her dates smelled her vulnerability like vultures circling roadkill.

When my phone rang and Tina's name showed up in my caller ID, I confess to recoiling. I assumed it was a crisis, usually a significant one. I knew she'd only call me as a last resort, and she had plenty of occasions to do so. I'd summon my courage and fortitude from her, because as I looked at what she was going through, I withered. We both laughed at the few times she'd call with news that wasn't crisis-related. I marveled at her stamina.

Tina is a classic example of the impact of stress on physical and mental health. After her family moved into permanent, subsidized housing, their troubles didn't cease. She was hospitalized several times for stress-related symptoms. This meant that her then-6 little boys needed care from someone else. She patched together arrangements with friends. Her kids learned how to fend for themselves. The fear of losing her children to foster care added unimaginable stress. One of the dads regularly threatened a custody battle. We finally figured out he did that around tax time so he could claim a dependent on his taxes. That he was woefully behind on child support payments didn't seem to faze him. Her shattered relationship with her mother, who lived nearby and who could have helped, underpinned Tina's anxiety. That, in turn, compounded the stress-related health issues she experienced. The inescapable consequences of the abuse she was subjected to as a child and adult certainly contributed to her deteriorating health.

During the years I helped Tina navigate bureaucracies, I developed a good working relationship with her housing authority caseworker, an unusual occurrence. Over the years, most government agency personnel, for any number of reasons, were unapproachable by someone like me advocating for a client. I admit to leaning on my role as a fierce national advocate with connections. I tried doing it in a way that would build, rather than burn, bridges. It kinda worked.

Fast forward 10 years from when I first met Tina and her family. After five or six years of poverty-related struggles in Las Cruces, Tina and her clan moved to a small town outside El Paso, Texas. A new apartment complex next to the school offered subsidized apartments and Tina qualified. Leaving her roach-infested trailer in Las Cruces was a no-brainer. She asked her housing authority caseworker for, and received, a modest amount of money to get resettled. Tina's supportive group of friends in Las Cruces helped the family move. She and her children, (including their latest arrival, a girl) flourished in this new setting. The boys excelled in school. Her oldest joined Junior ROTC, and welcomed the structure of military discipline. He worked a part-time job as he got older. Impressively, the boys' attendance was unblemished. They doted on their baby sister.

Then Tina met "Jose," a divorced father of three. He's a few years older than she. Unlike other relationships, this seemed destined to succeed. Tina, who loved animals and wanted to become a vet tech, grew up around horses. Jose's free time was spent in the local stables. Serendipitously, their mutual love of horses provided a foundation for a solid relationship.

Tina and Jose, and all the children, spent their spare time at the stables and participating in local rodeo events. Some would call it horse-therapy. They called it fun. Eventually Tina and Jose married and moved into a house in what can only be described as a "normal" neighborhood. Unbeknownst to those just seeing the house and blended family, they looked like they always lived in this thriving neighborhood. Tina became interested in photography. Jose crafted useful items out of horseshoes in his spare time. They began figuring ways to use their hobbies to earn a side income.

As of the writing of this book, things fell apart with Tina and Jose. She described repeated episodes of domestic violence. His physical and emotional abuse escalated during the last two years. As I finish this manuscript, Tina and her family are regrouping. Jose moved out. Tina demanded a divorce, accusing him of abuse and of infidelity.

Her and her family's world is still far from the various forms of homelessness she'd experienced in Las Cruces. It appears they'll be able to keep their subsidized housing.

The clouds of trauma cast darkness on their lives on occasion. Their resilience might help them weather this latest storm. They have a fighting chance to enjoy productive, healthy lives. Still, the family's proximity to homelessness haunts Tina, but she's resolute in her efforts to move forward. Despite this major setback with Jose, she and her children have support from a circle of friends. Their involvement with horses provides the therapy that helps them cope with their current and past struggles.

Tina's marriage woes underscore the vulnerability of parents with children. The need for companionship lures men and women into relationships. It's often difficult to discern the trustworthiness of suitors professing love. They are also desperate for someone for survival.

Tina's situation illustrates how no one "solution" will work for every family in a homeless situation, i.e. "get married." It reinforces the ongoing impact of the horrific episodes she encountered along the way. Hopefully, her determination, support of friends, and a minimal amount of outside assistance will keep them out of homelessness. I'm holding my breath.

Choose Your Hazard

These bumpy roads and dire warning signs require our intervention. Ignoring them imperils all of us. Helping families over these bone-jarring rough patches takes resources, stamina, and patience. Consider how tough the parents and kids are who endure such traumatic abuse.

The linchpin of assisting families experiencing homelessness is the school district's homeless liaison. They, along with other school personnel, can create miracles for the families. Their involvement conveys that the school genuinely cares. Their relationship goes a long way in supporting the family. When students succeed, as often happens, everyone wins. Removing the "road hazards" from the path of families often requires help. It's worth it.

Road Condition Report

Insufficient personal income and the lack of affordable housing are the major reasons for homelessness. Families may be impaired by complex, advanced medical problems. Psychiatric illnesses, sometimes exacerbated by drug and alcohol abuse; a lack of child care and transportation hamper economic recovery. These needs are challenging for health care systems, local communities, and the government. Solutions require more than a one-size-fits-all underfunded approach, such as HUD promotes. Yes, housing is a major part of the solution, but other assistance, tailored to a family's specific needs, must be available. When families hit rough patches, they often get blamed for losing their way when, in fact, the obstacle in their path was not of their choosing and was impossible to avoid.

"Choices," as in making bad choices, is one way critics dismiss a parent's circumstances. When, as a matter of fact, their decisions were not choices at all. One might choose a harmful mate because trauma affects judgment. Desperate situations may push the parent into a bad relationship to escape or avoid homelessness. A parent's drug use, abusive partner, or mental illness can create a rift. Involvement with the foster care system or child welfare authorities often comes at a price: upending living arrangements. Housing authorities have regulations banning certain ex-felons from the property, including those with a history of drug use. Property managers can impose arbitrary restrictions on who can visit. Ostensibly, these black-and-white rules are for safety. Often, these regulations unnecessarily cause homelessness, blemishing a parent's record so much that they are banned.

Choices are complicated. And we are not privy to what causes a person to make their decisions, so judging should be off limits. Families need options, not exile into homelessness.

The devastation of sexual abuse, whether as children or adults, creates mental and/or physical health issues that often haunt the person who was abused. Trauma from acts of violence can lead to self-medicating to numb the pain, difficulty maintaining healthy relationships or unstable housing. It exacerbates health problems, and creates turmoil that often impacts subsequent generations. The relationship between sexual abuse and homelessness, especially for women, requires much more study and a significant increase in long lasting support.

Rarely do I hear a parent or student talking about getting counseling to help them cope with the abuse they experienced. Think of it this way: if a car is in an accident and gets patched up enough to run again—the cheap "solution"—it might run again, for a short time. But you can bet it will break down at the worst time. How often do vehicles damaged in floods get cleaned up to look good and then sold to some unsuspecting buyer who discovers the inner damage after the fact? When I see junked cars—either littering neighborhoods or in massive junk yards—I think of how we "junk" people, letting them deteriorate instead of helping them survive and thrive. In no way do I mean to compare junked cars with people who have inherently more value. I do wonder why we don't put more effort into improving the opportunities for parents and kids to repair the damage done to them and to move down the road of life with a better chance of success?

I can't help but think about how we expect so much from women who have so little.

Don't make mistakes. Don't get misled by signs that someone loves you when they just want to have sex with you. Don't go down the road of wanting to have several children. Our demands on these moms are plentiful. Our genuine support is miserly. And we abandon them like a junked car on the side of the road.

An optimist is simply
a proactive realist.

- Vera Nazarian

CHAPTER 7
Check Engine

When I hop behind the wheel of my van, I normally have a destination in mind. If at all possible, I'll avoid interstate highways. If I'm really lucky, I'll get to pick a scenic route. But before I shove off for any extensive travel, I go through a mental checklist so I'm not stuck somewhere doing without something essential like food, water, or supplies. When I'm firing on all cylinders and I have an adequate wifi signal, I'll check weather conditions. I'll eyeball the obvious things on my rig, my tires, my fuel gauge and I'll clean my windshield.

Solo traveling, especially through the backroads, presents obvious risks. Cell phones don't always work in the hinterland, so the concept of calling for help is just a theory. As I ventured deep into the never-never-land of backroads, I did have occasional unnerving thoughts about mechanical breakdowns. The peace and joy of driving on roads where I could enjoy scenery and not wrestle with traffic usually quelled my fears. The other anxiety-producing thought was how expensive RV repairs are, coupled with the difficulty of finding a legitimate repair facility.

I learned the hard way. Ignorance is bliss, and expensive, when it comes to RV maintenance. With Tillie1, my biggest headaches centered around the generator, aka genny, the gas-fueled device that provided electricity when I was not plugged into an external power source. I didn't like using genny because of the noise, the cost and the environmental impact.

Maintaining a generator requires effort and attention, something I failed to do from early on. It cost me thousands over the years. You're supposed to run it for 30-minutes or so every week. I looked at that as a waste of fuel, money and an affront to the environment. I spent thousands on generator repairs. My frugal ways got expensive.

For the most part, my nine years driving Tillie1 were fairly disaster-free as far as maintenance. And when mechanical problems did arise, I was able to get them fixed without significant delay or expense. Overall, I'd say Ford and Gulfstream did a pretty good job building a reliable vehicle. After the odometer turned 200,000 miles, with fuel prices soaring out of control, I figured that the time was right to get a new vehicle. In 2014, I bit the bullet and decided on the Mercedes-Benz Sprinter as converted into living space by Sportsmobile. The main reason I bought this more expensive new RV, Tillie2, instead of a used one was reliability. That turned out to be a fallacy.

My choice of Mercedes-Benz and Sportsmobile has been dismazingly disappointing. From day one, my troubles with this high-end vehicle have vexed me. I've experienced mind-boggling deception and denial of responsibility on the part of Mercedes-Benz, a company I assumed had a commitment to quality. Sportsmobile, the company that outfitted the inside of the van, at least made efforts to repair the problems caused by their shortcomings.

Lest I give the impression of a totally-together traveler, I'm far from it. But I do what I can do when I can do it. I dunno, maybe it's a byproduct of my Girl Scout days of "be prepared" being drummed into my adolescent head. I'm pretty handy, though vehicle repair is beyond my scope of expertise. I can do minor electrical and maintenance repairs, but I rely on professionals for the big stuff. I responsibly follow regular maintenance schedules. I pay attention to unusual sounds and have them checked out. Evidently that's not enough.

My Nightmare Vehicle

When I bought this upscale van, Tillie2, I had great expectations for relatively trouble-free driving. Two weeks after driving off the lot, I became introduced to my new friend, the "Check Engine" light. It flashed ominous warnings, insisting that I "Visit Workshop." What workshop? It did so in the middle of nowhere South Dakota, on a Babes of Wrath trip with my friend Pat LaMarche.

We both were puzzled, even after looking through the owner's manual. I pulled over and we got out and looked at the tires (also pictured in the warning light display). They seemed OK. The vehicle drove fine. So, we carried on. But I wondered, and worried.

That was my introduction to what appears to be a lemon vehicle. Under warranty, Mercedes-Benz benevolently took me in and supposedly repaired the problem. I was on a first-name basis with Susan, my customer care rep at headquarters. Even she was flabbergasted by the frequency of my issues.

Once I blew past warranty, I was a persona non grata. Same problems. But now I paid dearly to have them fixed. And it seemed to me that "fixed" was relative. It meant temporary. Fix and repeat, often. The most common issue seems to be with the diesel exhaust system. I don't pretend to understand it, but a non-Mercedes diesel mechanic explained this issue as a chronic, expensive problem that will cause my "check engine" light to flash forever more.

I've kept an incident log and I've complained to Mercedes officials, all the way to the top. Letters, social media, phone calls. To no avail. And though I've only had this vehicle for 8 percent of my life, I've spent more time in MB waiting rooms than I have in doctors' office waiting rooms over my entire life. Don't get me started about the money!

Heads Up!

Dismazingly, not only did my vehicle give me mechanical trouble, the insides—the parts Sportsmobile installed—gave me my share of headaches. Almost literally.

In summer of 2018, Pat LaMarche and I were in California presenting at the national NOW (National Organization for Women) conference. Following that successful and invigorating event, we took a detour over to Yosemite.

I had been noticing a strange clatter coming from the living space. Hmmm. Not properly storing my stuff could cause a disturbing rattle. It was more than a coffee cup out of place. This new noise sounded serious. When we were getting settled into a campground for the night, I happened to look up, along the edge where the cabinets met the ceiling. I saw a huge gap between the two rear cabinets and the ceiling. Oh no! The cabinets, filled with my personal belongings and work stuff, were getting ready to rip themselves from the ceiling and crash onto our heads.

We beelined to a big box building supply store and I bought two shower extension rods. We wedged them under the cabinets. Stopgap, we hoped. I contacted Sportsmobile, who fortunately had an operation in nearby Fresno. They got me in and supposedly repaired it. A year later I had passengers riding in the back and the same thing happened: resulting in yet another trip to the Sportsmobile shop. That time in Indiana. They assured me they really fixed the problem. Why am I not reassured? My investment in two shower rods seems to be the best solution.

Even with resources, I find myself flummoxed by the out of the ordinary challenges life throws at me. What do families without resources do when worse things pummel them? My HEAR US journey revealed their resilience, resourcefulness, and intrepid spirit. To this day, they inspire me beyond words.

Safety Net Illusion

A major part of day-to-day survival depends on being able to afford the basics. I can, and I have a safety net—family and friends—who, I hope, would bail me out literally and figuratively if my world collapsed. When you can't afford what you need, you start operating on a moment-by-moment basis. Millions of families in America live in or on the edge of poverty, and therefore teeter close to homelessness. It's hard to feel like you can control what's down the road, or at least be prepared for it, when you can't buy your way out of a paper bag.

Living in the moment has value, but not when it causes a person's short-sighted decisions to negatively impact their well-being. That kind of involuntary, inadvertent tunnel vision haunts not only the short-term thinker but the broader community. Let me be clear—I'm not equating those who choose to live in the moment with those who didn't choose and are sucked into an impoverished lifestyle. The latter do the best they can with what little they have.

Disaster is often a series of unfolding events that intersect in a negative way.

Home(less)-Schooling Nomads

On my HEAR US 2020 VisionQuest trip—when I crossed the upper US on Route 20 (Boston, MA to Newport, OR, 3,365 miles) and I-20 (Florence, SC to just beyond Pecos, TX, 1,500 miles)—I met a nomadic family. Their lifestyle exemplified the "be prepared" mantra beyond what I could have imagined. "Sara" and her son "Kenny" (she requested that I not use their real names) lived in their little Honda SUV with barely enough room for one person, much less 2 people, a dog and cat.

Sara and I hit it off well from the get-go. And six-year-old Kenny just ignored me after he sensed his mom was fine with me and my video camera. I'm always tentative, not wanting to take advantage of a subject who might feel obligated to cooperate for whatever reason. So, I don't invade. Well, at least that's my intention.

I met this family the first time at an evening meal served by a local church in one of the larger cities on Oregon's scenic coast. The volunteers were, as I've seen so often, exemplary in their hospitality and their choice of menu. Full spread turkey dinner, even though it was October! These monthly gatherings offer an array of essentials—hygiene items, clothing, shoes. And for the kids—children's books, games, and small toys.

While Sara and Kenny were eating, I sat down and introduced myself. I had already been presented to the group by the school district's homeless liaison who escorted me to this extracurricular event.

As the two got more comfortable our conversation circled around their nomadic existence. Sara drew a diagram of how she arranged their little SUV. She had all the confidence of an interior designer explaining a blueprint to her client. I expressed interest in hanging around with them. She quickly agreed. We decided to meet Saturday morning. Sara said she'd text me their location. She wouldn't know until Friday night.

At the time, I was staying behind a nondenominational church. I'd stayed there before. The city has ordinances against sleeping in RVs and cars. What I was doing was technically illegal. I tried to be stealthy. I usually get away with such transgressions because I don't look like someone desperate enough to sleep in my vehicle or like I have nowhere else to go.

Sara texted me as promised. We made plans to meet up first thing Saturday morning. I wanted to film them crawling out of the car that chilly morning. They were parked in a quasi-municipal lot, a safe location, near a bathroom. Unfortunately, it wasn't unlocked until 8 am. Kenny stirred in his nest of blankets as I arrived. A typical 6-year old, he blurted out "Mom, I gotta pee." But first he had to find his shoes in the jumbled mess in the back seat.

As Kenny took care of business, Sara started re-ordering things. She looked for his soccer clothes and gear. He had a game that morning. She rummaged through stuff as she began unleashing their story of homelessness. She had an altercation with family. Now they're estranged. She and her husband split when she accepted that he was a ne'er-do-well.

Sara and Kenny traveled a lot, staying in some places longer than others. It depended on their accommodations and the community's tolerance for out-of-towners. They spent time exploring local attractions, turning those moments into educational experiences. She liked where she and Kenny landed on the scenic Oregon coast. But life was far from perfect.

"I found the less you care in life, the happier you'll be," she proclaimed somewhat carefree considering her vast list of concerns. Her motherly instincts seemed pretty sharp, cheering for Kenny while he and other 6-year-olds do what they do on soccer fields— chase around somewhat aimlessly. She hugged him when he got off the field. She played soccer with him on the sidelines during halftime.

As she and Kenny went through their nighttime routine, settling into their home-on-wheels outside a church, Sara announced, "We're reading Spiderman tonight," with no hint of monotony from the countless times she'd already read the book aloud to her snuggled-in son.

Their nomadic life came with practical challenges. Her road-worn SUV developed serious mechanical problems, not in the budget. The pets required shots and licenses, not in the budget. The storage unit monthly rent, $60, needed to be paid or they'd get locked out and lose all their stuff. Gas prices were over $3 a gallon. Driving was a luxury. Still, she had a 6-year-old with no real sense of how dire their circumstances were.

When I left them, and the coast of Oregon, I kept thinking about their world. I agonized over the weather reports that indicated a massive storm, bringing cold, winds and rain. I knew they were resilient and had been through this kind of stuff before. But I still worried. So, I called her. I told her the film I made of their situation was coming along nicely. And I asked how things were going.

Sara's car was creating some consternation. She and Kenny were temporarily bunking with a friend. They had to figure out options. She had to get enough money to fix their SUV. Fortunately, Kenny's school worked well with families in homeless circumstances. But they probably couldn't kick in for the cost of repairs. What do desperate parents do?

I had no illusions about the tentative nature of their doubling up. It's a misunderstood arrangement by the homelessness policymakers, thinking it's a safe, secure situation. Far from it, in most cases. It might start out as a friendly offer, but tensions quickly come into play. The "walking on eggshells" mantra understates the peril and vulnerability facing many, including the stoic Sara with her son. Some just up and leave when things get tense: a rash decision that is sometimes better and sometimes worse than staying.

Families know when they're not wanted. It might erupt as a fight over who drank the last of the orange juice, or more devastatingly when the host demands sex to stay. Or anywhere in-between.

As I left the coast of Oregon behind, my similarity to Sara and Kenny got real. My check engine icon lit up on my Sprinter dashboard, and it added a message that upped the ante, "10 starts remain." What the heck did that ominous message mean? The frequency of my check engine light flashing at me had numbed me to the potential for harm. The 10 starts thing meant just that—I could stop and start 10 times. Then it would then lock down, rendering me motionless. Time to find a damn Mercedes dealer. The bane of my existence!

Fortunately, I was near Portland, Oregon. I located an authorized dealer. Unfortunately, it would require three days to repair, pushing me to make other arrangements for sleeping and getting around. The $4,200 repair bill bit big time. Especially because this repair was caused, from what the repair advisor told me, by the broken bracket that I had spent $800 to repair less than a year ago. My frustration with Mercedes-Benz reached a peak I didn't think possible. But they wanted no part of accountability. It was all on me.

Car repairs spell disaster for any income-challenged family "fortunate" enough to own a vehicle, typically a beater. They buy from someone who promises them a great deal. If they buy from a car lot, and get a loan, the interest rate runs through the roof. A missed payment means the repo man shows up and yanks their only transportation out of their driveway.

Disaster Warning Lights

The tough decisions families face with vehicles usually center around repairs. Their approach is money-based. Car repairs aren't cheap. A few communities have developed nonprofit car repair operations, but very few. People like Melissa N, whose family lives miles from the center of their little town in north Florida, negotiated repairs with her mechanic ex-boyfriend. They had broken up, but remained friends. He kept thinking that his mechanical services would result in her intimate services. She had to scrape funds together to buy parts, including brakes, but she put the brakes on his advances along the way. In the meantime, her autistic teen son needed a ride to school, a 25-mile jaunt that she had to make twice a day.

I've known this stalwart mom 15 years. Prior to our meeting, she and her kids experienced homelessness several times because of what a single mom needs to do when the father doesn't contribute to support his offspring. She'd work as many flexible under-the-table jobs as possible while navigating the inevitable sick child call from the school nurse. She and her family bounced from motel to friends back to motel. They had stayed in a shelter that had a time limit designed to prevent families from getting too comfortable.

Our paths connected for the first time in January 2006. Melissa's kids were my first interviews. I approached this task with outward calm and inward anxiety because other than the power and record buttons, I knew nothing about my fancy video camera. Melissa, and her daughters, then 13 and 10, welcomed me with open minds. They were happy for the opportunity to share their stories.

As I interviewed these astute girls, Melissa cared for her son. Back then he was about a year old. Melissa later found out he suffered from autism. During the interview, we sat on the government-issued furniture in their barren "living room" that blended into their stark kitchen ala FEMA-cheap house trailer style.

The girls' level of insight about their living situation, and their cogent ways of describing the ups and downs, awed me. "I want to be the first woman president," declared the 10-year-old without a hint of bluster. She pointed out the pitfalls of homelessness, "You make new friends. Then you have to move again."

The one thing that both of my interviewees agreed on— school was important. It gave them a sense of stability. Their district, whose homeless liaison arranged for me to meet Melissa and her family, excelled at helping families and youth in homeless situations. As I've seen over the years, not all districts operate the same.

The family had been enjoying a period of relative stability in their own apartment when Hurricane Ivan hit (2004) and ravaged the Florida Panhandle. Their "apartment got mold and the landlord wouldn't fix it," declared the oldest girl in matter-of-fact tone that bore no shame. FEMA stepped up, offering families a time-limited haven in the form of an economy model single-wide house trailer.

Their trailer park sat on the outskirts of a naval base, a good 20 minutes from the little town of Milton where life happened. Most of the other trailers were occupied by Ivan refugees, too. FEMA trailers. One sneezed and the walls shook. These rattletrap structures also had a problem with formaldehyde, a toxic gas emitted from the haphazard way the materials were fabricated in those emergency dwellings. But it was home, at least until the April 2006 deadline for eviction, according to Melissa.

I remember leaving there after this debut experience— dismazed. I needed to learn what I was doing—fast. But in the meantime, I knew I was onto something. These young people were incredibly articulate, offering a compelling narrative about homelessness from the viewpoint of those often ignored—kids. The weight of this endeavor rested on my shoulders, sometimes like a sack of cement, sometimes like a pair of wings.

Little did I know that my contact with Melissa's family would continue through many years and tears.

What Fuels My Engine

It's important to understand why I'm doing what I'm doing—making these videos that let kids and parents experiencing homelessness educate viewers about the importance of school and what homelessness is like. My films, starting with *My Own Four Walls*, are widely used to expose educators (and others) to what family homelessness really means from the perspective of the students and parents. No more powerful awareness-raising tool exists!

HEAR US started out with a simple concept—I'd travel to non-urban places, film my interviews of children and youth sharing their experiences of homelessness, compile the interviews into a film and, viola! I learned my simple plan was anything but simple. This endeavor required more of me than I could have imagined. But 15 years later I'm still glad this was the path I chose.

Of the worthwhile things I've done in life, removing barriers that homeless kids encounter when they try to enroll in and succeed in school sits on the top of the pile. I continue to be inspired by my dedicated sisters and brothers in this movement, from my Washington, DC, national advocate-friend Barbara Duffield, to small, remote school district liaisons I've met during my travels. Their unfaltering efforts to ensure educational access for our nation's homeless students is inspiring! Their feedback about the usefulness of my video projects gives me strength to carry on when I feel like quitting.

The reaction I get from my interviewees really fuels my engines! Their love for their children's McKinney-Vento rights makes all I've done for this cause worthwhile. I can't count the times that my flagging spirits got a boost from something a student or parent says about their access to school. It's like a fuel-additive!

What is the Scope of Family/Youth Homelessness?

Few people have a grasp on the extent of this issue. Distorted statistics reported in the media, using HUD's understated estimate of homelessness, make it seem like homelessness is not that bad, "only" 500,000 or so are without homes. Rarely does a story dive deeper into the numbers to show how families, youth and many adults are excluded in HUD's census.

I am constantly dismazed about the media's lack of awareness of family homelessness. Geez! I, and a legion of passionate advocates, hammer at this issue constantly. We've developed strict criteria for defining and counting families and youth experiencing homelessness. The McKinney-Vento Education for Homeless Children and Youth Act contains realistic standards for identifying and counting students without homes. Even so, many students get missed for a variety of reasons. School personnel don't always recognize the signs of homelessness. Families are reluctant to report their lack of housing, fearing it may bring the child welfare authorities into their lives. And some don't recognize their situation as homeless. They're just going through "hard times."

My contribution to this conundrum is HEAR US. Our videos, books and presentations illuminate the magnitude of this issue. The greater the understanding of how many babies, toddlers, children and youth are without a place to call home, the more enlightened our response will be. That's the theory. And it tends to work in most places.

Having focused primarily on non-urban homelessness in my travels, I've been shocked at how many families are in various stages of homelessness. Shocked. Even me. The other shocker? How few places families can turn for help. Schools provide the lion's share of assistance, through the McKinney-Vento program and other avenues to serve economically-challenged families. Their contributions are good, but the problem far exceeds the best efforts of schools.

What if I told you that our nation has far in excess of 6.5 million children and youth experiencing homelessness? And that's a conservative estimate, pre-covid19. Those of us working in this field aren't surprised with that number. Dismazed, yes. People unfamiliar with this issue probably won't believe that number.

Here's a breakdown I did based on available hard data. It includes what we know about how many kids are not counted in the inadequate data collection. For the sake of the skeptics, this chart, which is on my HEAR US website, gives you a choice of estimates—including those unidentified, as I believe should be, and not including them.

HOW MANY CHILDREN/YOUTH ARE HOMELESS IN THE U.S.?

SUBGROUPS OF CHILDREN, YOUTH AND YOUNG ADULTS	ESTIMATED NUMBER	SOURCE
Identified in school (PK - 12)	1.5 million	http://profiles.nche.seiservices.com/ConsolidatedStateProfile.aspx
Babies/toddlers (0 - 5 yo)	1.5 million	https://www.schoolhouseconnection.org/young-children-experiencing-homelessness-an-overview/
Unaccompanied youth (13 - 17)	700,000	https://voicesofyouthcount.org/wp-content/uploads/2017/11/VoYC-National-Estimates-Brief-Chapin-Hall-2017.pdf
Unaccompanied young adults (18 - 25)	3.5 million	https://voicesofyouthcount.org/wp-content/uploads/2017/11/VoYC-National-Estimates-Brief-Chapin-Hall-2017.pdf
Under-identified in schools*	1 million+	https://www.schoolhouseconnection.org/public-schools-report-over-1-5-million-homeless-children-and-youth/
Estimated total infants young adults identified	7.2 million	Doesn't include parents/guardians
Estimated total infants – young adults including under-identified*	8.2 million	

Another way of figuring, 4%, a conservative estimate, of 50 million school kids = 2 million experience homelessness.

That doesn't include the little ones and the bigger ones not in school.

(HEAR US Inc., 2020)

First, one common truth within the entire homeless population: Millions of kids and adults have all lost housing due to crisis.

Family homelessness doesn't come in a one-size-fits-all model. So, one-size "solutions" don't work. Many communities I've visited barely have emergency family shelters. Many just open during cold weather. They haven't begun to develop an extensive array of housing stock and the corresponding services needed because funding is inadequate.

Historically, since the early 80s, in what we call modern homelessness, families have been all but ignored. I can remember my earliest days trying to learn more about family homelessness. Jonathan Kozol's book, *Rachel and her Children*, blew me away. But that was about families in New York City and the year was 1988. Other information, or advocacy efforts, didn't seem to exist. Family homelessness has exploded since then, impacting rural communities, small towns, mid-sized cities, and urban areas.

What's Wrong?

I'd love to ask Nan Roman, head of the National Alliance to End Homelessness: *How does family homelessness continue to increase?* As I've pointed out previously, one key factor is HUD minimizes it by their narrow definition of homelessness excluding most families. Those doubled up or staying in motels on their own dime aren't considered homeless by HUD. They're not eligible for HUD housing assistance. The US Department of Education's definition of homelessness includes doubled up and those staying in motels. HUD's denial of homelessness gets transmitted to Congress every year in the Annual Homeless Assessment Report (AHAR). As we moved into the 2020 decade, the number of homeless persons reported to Congress hovered around 500,000, certainly a problem worth addressing. What few realize, including those media outlets constantly using this number, is that HUD does not include families, youth or individuals who fall outside the narrowing definition of homelessness. While that sounds esoteric, consider the reality. The U.S. Department of Education reported in 2019 that approximately 1.5 million students were identified as homeless in schools across the land. That doesn't include parents, younger and older siblings, or youth on their own not in the school system. That number is severely undercounted.

But Congress hears that we've "only" got about 500,000 homeless people—mostly adults with physical/mental health issues and addictions. They don't hear about the kids, families and others who don't fit HUD's definition. No big deal. No big appropriation. This has gone on for three decades. Dismazing!

I can recall meeting with HUD officials—regional and national—in the 1990s, trying to convey the desperation of families in homeless situations. My viewpoint reflected my experience as a shelter director. I had no clue about the extent of the issue. I was appalled as I began traveling under my HEAR US banner. Finding and interviewing families and young people all over the country, in rural and suburban areas, I began to sense the scope and breadth of homelessness. It horrified me.

My HEAR US efforts to call attention to this issue have largely been videos. I've filmed and published close to 100 short videos of compelling interviews and footage. It took a while, but finally the positive aspect of "viral" took hold. Now the truth is being shared internationally. The films' spokespersons, those who've experienced homelessness, do an incredible job describing not only the agonizing parts of their lives, but also conveying hopes and dreams. Courageous parents and kids give voice and visibility to a mostly obscure population. If only we could force our government officials to sit and binge watch these videos. This economic and social injustice would be fixed in a heartbeat.

'Models' of Homelessness

Just like car models, with infinite differences and features, homelessness comes with a wide variety of aspects that often get lost in discussions and articles. Stereotypes abound, mostly centered on the male addict standing on street corners panhandling. Nothing could be further from the truth.

To be clear, I care deeply about the single individuals struggling without homes. I spent many years working with them. I'd love to go back and ask one simple question—did you experience homelessness as a child? I'd bet my lunch money that many did. Maybe they didn't know what to call it. Maybe they just attributed it to weird parents. To poverty. Or to going through hard times. But from what I've heard, this is a more common occurrence than anyone realizes. This would be a helpful piece of information to develop.

Having well-known figures share their stories can call attention to, and validate, ordinary peoples' experiences. Two stories I've read of celebrities whose "weird parents" dragged them through homelessness as kids, are Jeannette Walls and Misha Collins.

Glass Castle, an intriguing memoir by Ms. Walls, was published in 2005 as I prepared for my maiden journey. Jeannette's description of childhood experiences and her relationship with her parents stood out as something many people wouldn't describe as homeless. But was.

Misha Collins, an actor on the TV show "Supernatural" (which I've never seen) wrote a column for the New York Times. In "Even Without a Home, We Always Had a Family Meal," Misha describes his family's nomadic lifestyle. Again, maybe not seen as homeless. But was.

Families' experiences of homelessness can vary, and can include varying arrangements: from streets, to shelters, to motels, to vehicles, and doubled up. Families typically include single moms with kids. But two-parent families or dads with kids are also part of it.

Some families are homeless just a short time, lucky to make a quick escape. This usually requires just a little help. Some will bounce in and out, living on and off the edge so that the least little crisis will push them over. Some have been homeless most, if not all, of their lives.

Professor Yvonne Vissing, lead author for the textbook *Changing the Paradigm of Homelessness*, and I agreed that the phrase "going through hard times" fits many families. It's often how they describe their situations, maybe not wanting to use the label "homeless," or not knowing it applies. My heart aches for anyone who ends up without a home. No matter how long. I can guarantee that anyone who has been homeless does not want to return, but now returning is easier than ever.

'Going Through Hard Times'

Forever etched in my mind: An episode when I, with a student's mother, disputed the school's decision to deny her daughter's enrollment. This was pre-HEAR US at a prestigious high school in the Chicago suburbs.

I was working with Chicago area school districts to get them on the right track with the fairly-new McKinney-Vento Homeless Education Act. The district's registrar refused to enroll a new student. Her mother contacted Project REACH, the program I started and ran, and asked for help.

The mother and daughter lived in another state. They had stayed with the mother's ailing father and took care of him until he died. After his death, they moved to the suburban Chicago district because the mom's sister lived here. The sister took the family in, knowing they didn't have the resources to get their own place. When the mom went to register her daughter (the registrar was serving as the homeless liaison, an inappropriate duty), she was asked to produce documents normally required—a lease, utility bill, tax document, etc. She had none of that. Why not? She was staying with her sister. The registrar sent them away, school-less. Later, I went with the mom and listened as she again told the registrar they were *going through hard times*.

Too bad the registrar didn't connect with that phrase enough to ask a few discreet questions (asking privately and sensitively):

- What brought you to the decision of living with your sister? Do you have plans to move into your own place? Is that going to work out for you (i.e., do you have the financial resources to do so)?
- What was your situation where you were living before coming here? When you were staying with your family member in your previous state would you have been able to afford your own place?
- What was going on in your life before you came to this area as far as housing and independent living?

We managed to get the denial rescinded and the student was able to enroll. Immediately! Our program succeeded at reversing 100% of these decisions during the two years I ran it. (I've often wondered if that is why I was shown the door.)

Family homelessness is complicated. You can read our *Paradigm* book for more details. Hopefully my stories here, in

Dismazed and Driven, will give you insights as to the extent of, and impact of family homelessness.

One thing for sure: Getting into homelessness is easier than getting out of it.

Warning: System Failure

I keep thinking nothing will shock me.

In 2018, when Babe of Wrath Pat LaMarche and I headed to San Jose, California to do our presentation on "Sex for Stay" at the national NOW conference, we made time to swing through Silicon Valley. With all the global tech giant corporations located in that area, one might think that homelessness would be under control. That could not be further from the truth.

In most other areas, I'd see a few RVs that I'd figure were full-time campers - though not by choice. They'd usually be scattered discreetly in industrial areas, or stuck behind houses. In Silicon Valley, we saw blocks and blocks of a wide mix of campers. All, somewhat bedraggled, parked in neighborhoods of million-dollar homes. At one point I pulled over and filmed an entire long block of RVs of all kinds of shapes, not hooked up to water or electricity. Just there.

This aspect of homelessness causes increasing consternation. My sense is it's more about having these vehicles tarnishing lovely neighborhoods than being concerned about the suffering of those relegated to this unnatural lifestyle.

College and university campuses wrestle with the requests of students, some with kids of their own, who want to park and sleep on campus properties. Wrap your mind around that! Working on a college degree while sleeping in your vehicle: the new "normal."

Families living in mobile housing, most about 100-150 sq. ft. of total space, are doing so because they can't afford somewhere to live. They often have a history of evictions, bad credit, utility arrearages, felony records (mostly nonviolent crimes), and other blemishes that make them rental pariahs. So, they glom onto a cheap motorhome and find a place to park it.

RV campgrounds charge serious rent. They are out of the question for these families. Some RV parks don't allow older rigs. They cater to the multimillion dollar Class A RVs that offer a luxurious lifestyle for the upscale nomads. Parking in municipal areas often runs afoul of local ordinances. Campers can get ticketed and towed. In Berkeley, and other communities, reluctant officials open up areas for campers. But those fill quickly.

Unauthorized Camping USA is just one example of the spectacular failure to address homelessness. Silicon Valley, with unimaginable resources, caused the housing crisis that balloons on their streets. They could do something about it.

But this issue is not just out west.

Veteran, His 3 Sons and Greta

In Mobile, Alabama, in 2012, I met Jason, a veteran. He was living in a small camper with his three teen-aged sons and their adorable dog, Greta. They welcomed me into their world. Jason gave me a tour while his sons stood by. Living in a camper myself helps erase the gaps of shame. Their camper, holding four guys and a dog, was smaller than Tillie1. Theirs was an old, leaky model with much wrong with it. It wasn't used for travel, so that helped. Their shower didn't work, which gave them more storage space.

The campground they lived in cost $400 a month. Relatively cheap, but it offered nothing special except a safe place to park their "home." Jason worked. The boys went to school.

Greta, their small Schnauzer, guarded their empire. Unbeknownst to many, Mobile gets more rain than Seattle, making the leaky flaw of their RV a factor that caused more than just a minor inconvenience. Some things I know from experience. I've had my share of leaky roofs.

We've come to accept these alternative, inadequate living conditions as normal. We think it's okay for a family of four to cram in space made for one or two, to live hand-to-mouth, to worry about eviction and other upheavals. We have watched the standard of living soar into the stratosphere for the so-called one percent, while the bulk of the American populace struggles to survive abject poverty.

I call foul. The nation's "check engine" light is flashing. Time for a drastic overhaul. Lucky for you, America, I'm your homelessness mechanic.

Determination, energy, and courage appear spontaneously when we care deeply about something. We take risks that are unimaginable in any other context.

– Margaret J. Wheatley

CHAPTER 8
Takes a Toll

I can wax eloquently about the perks of a gig like mine. I see beautiful places, can work by a peaceful stream, sleep as I hear waves rolling in, and more. Sharing the downsides rubs me a little raw.

We are all social beings, or so we think. I enjoy solo traveling, most of the time. But I've had moments of being lonely. *Does anyone care that I'm out here doing this craziness?* Being out on my own? Doing a project that I wanted to do? One that didn't seem to mean anything to anyone else? At times those questions would hit me like stones on my windshield. Not often. Not often enough to make me quit. But it takes a toll.

The other aspect of my nomadic life that takes a toll is not having a place I can call my own. I'm not sure what that would look like anymore. I've pondered it over many miles. We all long for a place of our own, in some form. I envision something small. I don't have money for anything too extensive, nor would I want to sink my money into a traditional house. Nor do I see myself renting a traditional apartment. But I've learned to never say never.

People generously invite me to stay in their homes when I am looking for a place to park. I appreciate their hospitality. As I was devising this unconventional journey, I decided that my home on wheels would be my home. I didn't want to travel in a car and stay in motels. My solution—my house on wheels—was the only way I could pull this off. I wanted to sleep in my own bed, surrounded by my stuff, spartan as it may be. Stay in your driveway? Yes. Stay inside your home? Generally, no. Parking in other people's driveways made it possible to do this project on the cheap. And I've made some awesome friends in the process!

My occasional turmoil when parking and staying for a few days or more at someone's home contains a few issues. First, I must convince some that I am really fine with my choice. That it's no reflection on their housekeeping or choice of mattress, or anything. Sometimes it's a cat. I'm allergic. But it boils down to I wake up early (4:30 - 5). I generally like going to bed early (between 9 and 10). I don't like TV—mostly the ads, but probably the programing if I had to guess. I like quiet and minimal light to start and end my day. I have my own coffee and fixings and have gotten really stuck on my eating regimen. I'll bend on the food, and sometimes the coffee routine, but that's about it.

One peril of homelessness that I've come closer to understanding is doubling up. When a family loses their place to live, they often end up bouncing around with others—family, friends, or acquaintances. The host makes sacrifices. They give up their routines and space, sharing food and utilities, and often wondering when their "company" will leave. Anyone who's had company that stayed too long can relate.

In many cases, a kind person will offer to take in a family, but do so without checking their own lease. Who knows where their lease is? Why would they think they can't be nice to someone? That this invitation frequently comes from someone who has been, or is close to being, homeless is no surprise. This sort of host family is vulnerable to losing their housing just for being kind. Public housing residents have limits on how long visitors can stay. Visitors generally have to pass a background check: meaning no major felonies or sex offender status. If the public housing resident allows someone to visit in violation of their lease, they can be evicted. So too can tenants with visitors in private leasing agreements.

The invader, er, guest comes with baggage: literal and figurative. If it's a family, the kids present endless challenges to the parent and to the host. That's just the way kids are. The parent, likely under a tremendous amount of stress on a good day, agonizes over noise, mess, food, laundry, and more. The kids can't be kids. Stuff breaks. Bathrooms are rarely unoccupied. Too much bandwidth gets used. TV is too loud. No privacy. And so much more.

This is a common topic when I've interviewed families. "Walking on eggshells" (as if anyone has ever tried that) is a phrase used by practically every parent I've talked to when they describe the difficulties of being doubled up. I get it.

A few places I frequent for extended periods of time have given me glimpses into the doubled up quandary. People—my friends and family—have their sense of order, so I try like crazy not to leave my stuff around. I'm pretty much a minimalist by necessity, but I do have stuff. If I'm working on film editing, my computer and external drives spread out over the table. I'd like to leave them, but I best not. Even chairs perplex me. People have their chairs. Showers. Laundry. All the things I'm told they're happy to have me use come with unspoken protocol. I, too, have learned the art of walking on eggshells.

But I'm an adult with modest means and options. I can leave. Families doubled up are usually stuck in their situation no matter how crappy it gets.

I've known families that have endured more than crappy. It's been downright dangerous. Life-threatening.

Beyond Crappy

Melissa T has shared her story publicly because it will help others. She believes it and so do I. Her homelessness, with her two young girls, started as so many do, with a divorce. The girls have two different fathers (a phenomena not limited to impoverished parents). When she first became homeless, a friend offered to take them in. When Mel (I call her Mel) saw the closet-like space that was going to be their "room," Mel decided that having two girls to care for would be detrimental for everyone involved. She asked the father of her oldest if he'd take care of their daughter until Mel got back on her feet.

That's a tough thing for any mother to do. Under the circumstances it seemed like the right thing—kind of a "Sophie's Choice" where the mother needs to decide which child lives so that both won't die. Doubling up and splitting up are fairly common dilemmas for a mother (or dads with custody) when too many children become impossible to care for. Child protection services might get involved. Or the parent may just make a stress and poverty-fueled decision to divide the family.

When I met Mel in 2015, she and her youngest girl, Hanna, were living in the podunk town of Hope, Kansas. When I say living, they were staying at the home of a wheelchair-bound man. Mel was providing basic home care in exchange for a small room with a bed and dresser.

I could have predicted what would come next. This man made it clear that he wanted Mel to service him in ways far beyond health care. She refused, but was unnerved by it. She knew enough about sex abuse from personal experience to be extremely protective of her young daughter. Mel slept with scissors under her pillow. Her lack of trust came from previous incidents when male-hosts decided they could demand sex-for-stay.

For the two to three years Mel and her daughter spent homeless prior to 2015, they had been through the roster of bad situations. Typically, a "kind" man would offer his extra room. Sooner rather than later it would become clear that sex was part of the expectation. Mel would refuse, often getting beaten in the process, and they'd be homeless again.

The one shelter in the area that accepted moms and kids was the kind of place that I've heard about from families across the country. The rules and procedures were prison-like. As someone who spent years running a shelter, I can understand the need for rules and procedures. I draw the line at the extreme practices that defy any sense of hospitality and destroy any semblance of dignity and self-worth.

The other aspect of shelters that present a hardship: Time limits. I'm constantly dismazed at the organizations that profess to help homeless families but limit their stay to two weeks or some arbitrary time period. Even in good times, with low housing occupancy rates and plenty of assistance for families trying to find their own place, two weeks is insufficient. (In my lifetime, I've never seen anyone move out of homelessness in two weeks).

When Mel and her daughter moved into the shelter, the clock began ticking, increasing the pressure on this already stressed-out mom. When one of the other residents at the shelter offered a place to stay, she desperately accepted.

She assured me, and I believe her, that she didn't take those arrangements because she wanted to sleep with the guy. I've seen her around her daughter over the years. I've spent a lot of time talking with her. The idea of sex for stay isn't her thing – she learned the hard way – long before she ever moved to Hope in the first place.

Before she moved into Hope (or Hope-less, as she aptly called it), she navigated an arrangement that ended up with physical abuse because she refused sex. Her hand was smashed in a door as she tried to close it to keep him away. She desperately turned to Craigslist and found what she hoped to be a genuine offer from a man who claimed to be a pastor. But that took an ugly turn. That's when Mel and her daughter escaped to Hope.

I've encountered a dismazing number of invisible women with kids. They're doubled up in a nothing-going town like Hope. Family homelessness in small towns and rural communities has an entirely different look compared to urban areas. No shelters, no human service agencies, and no way out. People are stuck.

Mel described what life was like there. The library was seldom open. They had limited computer access. No grocery stores. No gas station or convenience store. Pretty much nothing except a public school. At least her daughter was allowed to enroll without difficulty. The school was aware of the McKinney-Vento Act guaranteeing educational access for students despite their homelessness.

The other thing that many women have in common is the joint debt incurred when they were married or together with their partner. That millstone follows them and, in many cases, it becomes the barrier to future housing: public or private. After Mel's ex left her with a cloud of debt, she let her mom move in, hoping it would help with both their living expenses. Things fell apart and Mel left. Then her mother ran up about $2,500 in rental debt before she was forced out by the landlord. If Mel wanted an apartment, that debt needed to be paid. That wasn't likely for someone in Mel's situation. She faced a double-whammy of debt.

Besides constantly rebuffing her predatory landlord, Mel had an income problem. Despite what many people still think about single mothers getting a fat welfare check, Mel didn't. Nor do most who could really use a little cash each month. The paltry child support payment of $100 a month from Hanna's father was it. Food stamps varied depending on Mel's income, but typically about $150 or less per month. She became an expert at getting by on next to nothing. Over the years, it hurt her to see how her daughter suffered because of this.

Mel's college education and professional work experience did her no good in a small town with 339 inhabitants. Escaping Hope wouldn't be easy. Even using her cell phone was challenging. It only worked if she stood outside. Any job would have to be flexible because she had to be "home" with her daughter.

Her trauma-related health issues loomed not far in the background. Mel mused about jobs she theoretically might get. Like those she'd had in earlier years. Her fantasy jobs required physical strength and agility: balancing food trays, being on her feet for hours, lifting heavy boxes. In her next breath she'd shared her health concerns: spinal cord issues, joint problems, and heart trouble. When she spoke with me comparing her illusion with her reality, she'd pause. A depressing awareness would swamp her optimism. She would shake her head knowingly.

When I first met her, she had agreed to be interviewed for a film I was making about doubled up homeless families in Kansas, *Worn Out Welcome Mat.* We sat on the porch of her tormentor's house. He was conveniently away for a few hours. She unloaded her story: a common thing for women who haven't had anyone listen to them for a long time. Two hours later, my head was spinning and Mel was exhausted. I thanked her and promised I'd reconnect.

For most of the families I've met, their dire situations had some possibility of escape, some potential for good. Mel's, not at all. I was tormented. From my years of trying to help families escape homelessness, I could usually see a glimpse of a light. If nothing else, I'd recommend they call and talk to their Congressperson's constituent issues staff member. But here in conservative, Republican Kansas, she was out of luck.

I don't like the word impossible. Sometimes it takes a little longer to make something happen. In this case it did. Mel and Hanna languished in Hope for almost two years after we met. In that time, hopes were raised and dashed repeatedly.

Finally housing units in Manhattan, Kansas opened up. The housing authority sent Mel an application form. Her predator told her he wouldn't fill it out. He said she should complete the form and he'd sign it. She showed him the completed form. He signed it.

I found a donor to help pay her housing arrearages. Good. She owed hundreds in back utilities. Bad. I found a resource for those. Good. Mel submitted her application to the Manhattan Housing Authority. Good. She was tentatively approved. Very good. Her predator didn't want her to leave. Too bad. He pretended to be her "landlord" and called to rat her out. Awful bad. He said Mel forged his signature on the application, omitting the detail that he had her fill it out so he could just sign it. To make matters worse, a drug charge popped up on Mel's record. Whoa! Wicked bad. She was denied by the housing authority.

This saga continued for what seemed like an eternity. I urged Mel to appeal the application's denial. We even begged the housing authority officials for that. We were able to get the local homeless liaison, who knew Mel's situation and knew public housing application procedures, to go along to the appeal meeting.

The drug charge was seven years old, and was a nothing-burger. She agreed to pick up a prescription for her then roommate, not knowing the Rx was written on a stolen prescription pad. She admitted it when the police got involved, and she had gotten probation. She'd long since successfully completed her probation but the charge showed up on the application background check. The housing authority required that the probation officer sign a form verifying her story. Mel pawned her daughter's computer tablet to pay someone to drive her to get the probation officer's signature.

Oh, and at the meeting, Mel showed the housing authority director a letter written by her "landlord" that was clearly sexual in nature. It offered proof that this situation in Hope was far more than just a doubled up arrangement. Mel was finally granted permission to move in.

It took almost two years, with strong intervention by me on occasion, and close to $4,000 to clear up the mess from the past. How would this work for a family with similar obstacles and no advocate with resources and know-how?

Lest one think Mel had been through enough, and that moving into a nice little 3-bedroom unit of subsidized housing would let her reach for her dreams? No.

Because her ex bounced a few checks in their joint account, Mel couldn't get a checking account. You don't know how important checking accounts are until you don't have one. The Federal Deposit Insurance Corporation (FDIC) reported that in 2017 more than 32 million households were un-banked or under-banked. That puts economic transactions out of reach. You can't get a cell phone, make utility payments, or do a host of other essentials without a plastic card. Since the banks own the debit card industry, the un-banked person gets thrown to the wolves who prey on the plastic-deprived masses. Then the finance companies profit even more by charging exorbitant fees.

Mel had one of those non-bank cards from Walmart, and was charged a fee of $3 or more every time she used it, for deposit or withdrawal. It was killing her $100 a month budget. Sure, her rent was 30% of her monthly income, but the rest of her essentials demolished the balance. For a time, I paid her internet provider. I figured she'd eventually get a job and be able to pick that up.

I've been over to Mel and Hanna's place several times. Their frugal decor, thanks to Mel scouring thrift shops or finding freebies, doesn't look bargain basement at all. It's a cozy, welcoming environment that contrasts with the dingy room in Hope. Her housing stability is not something she takes for granted. And her homeless past is not something she forgets. It takes a toll on her every day.

Mel's troubles still weren't over. The impact of her prior debt from student loans surfaced like a voracious monster from the deep. Her consumer debt—the bounced checks by her ex, and a past due water bill—lured the rogue debt collectors. Some consumer debt gets written off. But instead of bygones being bygones, rogue credit collectors go after dead bills anyway. So called "zombie debt" zeroed out years earlier still technically exists. The zombie hunters pursued Mel like sharks smelling blood.

Mel showed me 3 official (State of Kansas agencies) documents regarding her debt. The short story is that in a previous lifetime, before she became homeless, she didn't pay a $94 water bill.

Seven years later, the collection agency sent a sheriff to deliver a summons for that bill (how much did that cost?). She wanted to pay her debt. In the process of a horribly nasty call, the collection agency rep told her that the water bill had grown to *at least* $275 (fees and interest). Mel also had unsettled debt with a bank. She still owed about $500, from 12 years earlier. A lifetime for her, that debt had risen to more than $700.

If you think you can't squeeze blood from a turnip, you should study these debt collectors. They managed to lock onto the measly, but significant, $900 payment Mel had coming to her for contract work with a local nonprofit. Before her deposit hit the bank, the money was taken in its entirety by the collection agency. Without warning. Her designs on this money hadn't been extravagant. Pay for some medication no longer covered by Medicaid. Get her daughter some essentials. Buy food. Pay her car insurance and maybe pay a friendly mechanic for much-needed repairs. Poof. It was gone.

For those who still have the mentality that debts need to be paid, that's a good theory. I challenge you to look into the debt collection industry and see how they have morphed into what might be considered organized crime-like in their operations. It's a cesspool that involves our nation's banking industry. Congress's complicity with this greedy industry is appalling and unabated. And creates and perpetuates homelessness.

I'm grateful to have met Mel. She's taught me with every one of these grueling episodes how homelessness takes a toll. Her lessons are painful because they help me see how insidious poverty and homelessness really are. A person thinks escape is possible, but then gets targeted by relentless forces, like debt collectors, or the criminal "justice" system, or countless predators who will ruthlessly rip the last nickel from their own mother's hand.

It takes a toll on me, too. I have a limited arsenal with which I can help families escape these exploiters. I know a few lawyers I can turn to. I am painfully aware that they can't provide me unlimited legal services, even though they'd like to. So many need their help. These nefarious debt collection businesses operate with impunity. No mercy. Even if they're wrong. It nauseates me when I help a family pay off a debt to these credit repair rip-off artists because the debt has already been written off. The slimy operators have paid pennies on the dollar to harass beleaguered debtors within an inch of their lives. Each repayment enables the practice to profit. These predatory collection agencies get to keep every dime they wrench from people like Mel.

Debt collectors take a toll on millions in hard-scrabble situations. People feel like they can't get a job because the money will never see the light of day. Credit repair, payment plans, and most of those theoretical solutions have been co-opted by legalized greed. Government agencies, like the short-lived Consumer Financial Board that Senator Elizabeth Warren shepherded, should offer protection, but they've been gutted by the Republican leaders determined to make America great again for those who are already too rich.

Yes, that's a rant. One that can be backed up by facts and data. Though not the purpose of this book. Mel's situation isn't an aberration. I've encountered similar horror stories, and have done reading and research on this topic. I am convinced that we will only make progress on homelessness if we address myriad issues that plague vulnerable families.

Get It Right!

I was so tired of hearing that homelessness was caused by mental illness and addictions that I put together a chart that depicts the other issues that keep families housing insecure. Hundreds of things that would thwart a strong, unstressed adult are laid out on this chart.

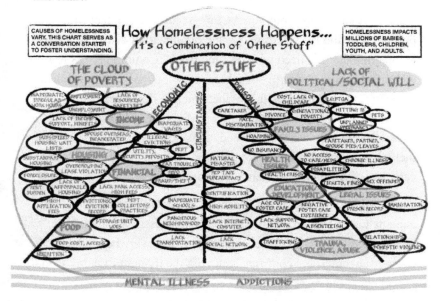

"Other Stuff" diagram created by Diane Nilan, HEAR US Inc. www.hearus.us   © HEAR US 2020

When we say homelessness takes a toll, that's an understatement. At least with tolls, after you pay, you can head down the road.

A big part of how homelessness takes a toll comes before a family becomes homeless. Again, I could not count the number of adults and teens who've shared that they've been abused as children, most of them sexually. Trauma, a by-product of abuse, takes a toll on the person who has been traumatized. It's not "just" mental, it's physical.

Multitudes of studies have documented the impact of trauma on a person's health. Chronic health conditions, like heart problems, diabetes, cancer and respiratory diseases are common. Clinical depression, substance abuse disorders, higher suicide risk add to the mix. The higher a person's ACE score (Adverse Childhood Experiences), the greater the risk.

What are the common ACEs? According to a fact sheet published by the Bassuk Center – and organization dedicated to helping the marginalized with housing needs, Common ACEs are emotional, physical and/or sexual abuse; emotional and/or physical neglect; household domestic violence; mental illness and/or substance abuse; parental separation or divorce; and having a parent/family member incarcerated. Outside the home, ACEs include economic hardship, community violence, bullying, foster care, and discrimination (racism, homophobia, etc.).

A trauma expert, Dr. Bessel Van der Kolk, offered a clear explanation of trauma, in an interview with Elissa Melaragno. Dr. Van der Kolk said: "Trauma is something that overwhelms your coping capacities and confronts you with the thought: 'Oh my God, it's all over, and there's nothing I can do. I'm done for. I may as well die.'" Death comes knocking for too many.

The End of the Road

I had never visited Mississippi before I started my HEAR US sojourn. I found plenty to like in that diverse state. Still, poverty and all that goes with it seem to overpower the good of the "Birthplace of the Blues." At the end of 2009, during my usual scan of news stories about family homelessness and poverty, a gut wrenching tragedy caught my eye. The town of Starkville had a fire just three days after Christmas. It took the lives of three women and six small children. I looked into the details of the story and got somewhat involved. Excerpts from my blog at the time, *invisible homeless kids*, tell it best.

1/11/10, invisible homeless kids blog

> *A family having "hard times" (translation, homeless because they lost their housing due to hardship) in Starkville, MS was taken in by a friend who understood what "hard times" does to a family, as she was not far from that pernicious condition. On Monday, Dec. 28, 2009, in Starkville, a fire rooted in poverty and overcrowded living space took their lives, three women and six small children.*

> *Having known "hard times," India Williams, a 25-year-old mother with three small children of her own, squeezed two other families into her humble apartment. I'm not sure of the exact circumstances, but having seen this tragic story unfold countless times, I would guess that a domestic*

*disturbance, money problems, and/or some
kind of neighborhood violence caused the
loss of housing.*

*The fire that took their lives, sadly, is
not unlike a mostly unnoticed nationwide
house fire epidemic (certainly getting less
attention than H1N1), as winter has frozen
even Florida. Local news reported that the
Red Cross estimated a 200% increase in
house fires in this country, and utility shutoffs cause a good number of those fires as
impoverished and desperately cold
households turn to unsafe methods to stay
warm. (Does your Red Cross do more than
put house fire survivors in a motel for just a
few days? Enlighten me.)*

11/22/10 **invisible homeless kids**
blog

*Deep South manners are the same,
no matter the state. "Yes ma'am, and ya'll
come back" punctuate most sentences. Such
is the case as I paid my fee at a little
campground outside Starkville, MS. I headed
into my meeting with Mayor Parker Wiseman
to talk about what's happened to protect
desperate families that lose housing.*

*Last December, fire swept through a
two-bedroom apartment in Starkville, taking
the lives of nine people crowded into the*

---

dwelling. Six children under the age of six and three women perished. Cause of the fire? Hard times.

After blogging about it, I met with Mayor Wiseman earlier this year when I was crossing Mississippi. Why not, I thought, because someone needs to make sure these women and kids didn't die in vain. My organization, HEAR US, collected money to help with burial costs. He graciously agreed to meet me, and by chance the Alderwoman who represents the family's district happened to be at City Hall, so she joined us.

We talked about resources and need. Mayor Wiseman had done his homework and was appalled at the gaping holes in the safety net. I wasn't. He vowed to bring stakeholders together to strategize how to avoid this tragedy, as best as possible, in the future. I vowed I wouldn't forget his promise.

So, I'm back. The economy has gone through another shellacking, or drubbing, or whatever you call it when the rich get theirs and nothing is left. Mississippi, according to a recent report issued by the National Center on Family Homelessness, ranks 41/50 on the problem of child homelessness. Their stats are a year-old. Things continue to spiral downward.

Winter hasn't hit with its bone-chilling fury, and when it does, the thousands of people in Mississippi who can't afford heat will do what any of us would do—figure out how to heat their humble abodes by any means possible.

The Cost of Tolls

I remember feeling gut-punched as I ruminated on this stark tragedy. The issue of house fires is one I've tracked over the years. I've been at the scene of several. Families lose their housing and struggle to get back on their feet. I've been in plenty of mobile homes, trailers, campers, and I've seen the slipshod construction. I've witnessed the piss-poor maintenance by the landlords renting these housing options.

Fire is a real danger, especially in flimsy structures. The speed with which flames race through these tinderboxes and the toxicity when they burn makes them the most dangerous housing available. Albeit the cheapest. Tornadoes and hurricanes can tear them up, too.

What seems to get overlooked is how little help is available for those who've lost their place to live, as humble as it may have been. My communications with members and volunteers in the Red Cross confirm that they are only able to provide a few days of help. I understand that. But what happens when the family hits the end of the road?

The Toll of Departure

Often, I pop in and out of locations, staying a short time and moving onto my next stop. But I do stay longer on occasion and that takes a toll on me. Usually, if I'm staying for a longer time in one place, it's at the home of someone special to me—family, close friends. I get used to being there, and feel (mostly) at ease with navigating the day-to-day rhythms of being in someone else's space.

When I have to shove off, I do what I need to do to be physically ready. I stock up on my vittles, etc. Being mentally ready? Well, that's another thing. I get sad. It's a separation thing—knowing I won't have that person around to enrich my day. When I left Mom, I'd wonder if I'd see her again. Knowing death is inevitable. As she hit her 90s her days were numbered. She quickly passed away in 2013.

Other loved ones have, as they say, crossed the bridge as I've been traveling. My Dad in 2008, which sent me scrambling cross-country from a conference to family to make the arrangements. My baby sis left us in 2009, leaving us all shell-shocked. My niece in 2018, a heartbreaker.

I guess my lesson has been I never know. Saying goodbye is tough. When I pull up stakes, which seems to be the toll I pay for nomadic living, I don't know what's down the road. The pain of separation stings.

A Grueling Task Before I Left Town

I had the honor of meeting "Alicia," a mother of three young children, just days before she died. They had stayed at the Hope Haven shelter in DeKalb, Illinois. It was run by a longtime friend of mine, Lesly Wicks. In October 2007, just before I headed west to film and make a series of presentations, Lesly asked if I'd film an interview with Alicia so her children would have a memory. Yikes! Of course. Yes. But the scope of this interview was far from what I'd imagined doing.

The first scheduled time for the interview needed to be rescheduled, Alicia was not feeling well enough. We put it off a few days. I connected with my friend Gary, the shelter manager. You'll meet Gary in Chapter 10. He's the guy who was scared to travel by his "Black-self" across the country. We went in and he introduced me to Alicia. I also met "Derrick," a friend of hers from the shelter, and her kids, ages 10, 6, and 3. The guys took the kids somewhere so we could have privacy.

Alicia sat on the couch, hooked up to oxygen. I tried to explain as gently as possible what I thought we should do. Having no clue how this was supposed to be done, I knew I needed to hold it together until I got out of her apartment.

This determined mother used her short time at the shelter to put the pieces back together after personal crises. She earned her GED, became certified as a nursing assistant, and got a job. Bingo! They moved out. All looked good. About two months before we met, Alicia called Lesly and said she was having trouble breathing. Lesly urged her to call the doctor and offered whatever support she could give.

Alicia's life swirled out of control. The doctor visit, heart surgery, and discovery of inoperable cancer brought changes she never expected. Was this trauma related? I can only suspect yes. The impact on her already-traumatized children agonized Alicia and all who knew and loved them. Alicia's sister lived in town and was willing to take the children.

Alicia struggled to talk, especially when speaking about her children. The entire interview lasted less than 10 minutes. We chatted while waiting for everyone to return. I'm not good at small-talk. When I saw her using toilet tissue on her nose I winced. *How can you use that sandpaper on your tender nose?* She laughed. I gave her a new box of Ultra Soft Puffs, my tissue of choice.

When Gary, Derrick and the kids came back, I left. It was a beautiful day for a drive in the country. I hadn't selected a route so I just headed in a general direction, north and west. I was numb. Alicia and her kids' faces stuck in my mind. This interview took a toll on me. Life took a toll on Alicia. And her family. She died about a week later.

I put the interview together and added music from a friend, Sara Thomsen, who wrote these lyrics and sings the song, *Holy Angels*. She gave me permission to share it with you too.

You are held by holy angels;
holy angels all around you.
Hush, now, sleep child,
sing the holy angels
We are holding you.
You can rest.
Morning will come, child,
The dawn will break through the darkness.
We are holding you
through the light of the newborn day.

Life is a hard battle anyway. If we laugh and sing a little as we fight the good fight of freedom, it makes it all go easier. I will not allow my life's light to be determined by the darkness around me.

- Sojourner Truth

CHAPTER 9
No GPS

Once I began to grasp how big this country was, I knew I needed to get a GPS. Hard to remember that in 2005 those devices were not built into our not-yet-in-existence smart phones. I made a tough decision to splurge for a high-end GPS, setting me back a painful $500.

I have always been a paper map gal. My atlas was my go-to navigation tool. I tried to adapt to the electronic gadget that promised to guide me across the backroads of America. The first test came early on, in the middle of Mississippi, where I had eyeballed a rural route that would've benefitted from additional guidance.

Maybe I hadn't been paying attention to the direction I was headed. That was an easy mistake to make when depending on early fickle technology. The impatient electronic voice ordered me to make a U-turn on a narrow 2-lane road. It demanded compliance as I replied aloud that I needed time to find room for my bigger vehicle to safely turn around. Once I completed that Tillie1-sized U-turn, I was more than annoyed to hear the voice chirp at me again that I needed to do a U-turn. Did I miss something? Dismazed, but obedient, I reversed heading again. My attention to the route heightened, but I was starting to lose what little sense of direction I had. The third turn-around command was the last straw for that damned GPS. I could get lost on my own, thank you very much. I rejected my first instinct to fling it out the window. Instead, I returned the device for a refund and went back to my old fashioned habit of using my atlas.

A discussion about paper maps vs. technology heats up about as much as Cubs vs. White Sox. My theory? A real map forces me to pay attention. It's more work. But it usually keeps me on the right path. When a tech device fails for whatever reason, I am lost. From my experience, I don't rely on my innate sense of direction when my electronic navigator is leading me. If it's cloudy I get "confused." Once I'm lost, it takes serious effort to get back on track. I do use my smart phone map app. Still, I tend to give the atlas a good check before setting out. I've learned to trust my instincts.

Really Lost

With all due respect, it's my strong belief that our executive branch, Congress and the heads of federal departments that impact families experiencing homelessness are, well, lost when dealing with homelessness and poverty. I'm bipartisan pissed. My assessment applies to current and past administrations. Sadly, it will likely apply to future leaders. Though I'll refrain from judgment of them until they prove otherwise.

I base my assessment on what I've seen over more than 3 decades. It's dismazing how we have stood by, politically, and twiddled our collective thumbs. Meanwhile the road under millions of vulnerable families crumbled, leaving them to fall into cavernous potholes of homelessness.

The steady predictable surge of families hitting various iterations of homelessness has increased since the mid-1980s. I agree with those who point the big finger at President Reagan's dismantling of programs serving vulnerable populations. He eviscerated HUD's budget. Until then, HUD had provided a semblance of housing assistance for the most vulnerable. Reagan's cuts inspired subsequent administrations to do the same. Those subsequent cuts created our current, unprecedented affordable housing crisis. President Trump's overt disregard for people in poverty and his racist stereotyping make the Reagan era look like a time of compassion.

In 1996, when President Clinton and his bipartisan brutes axed the previous shred of family support, aka welfare, even more struggling families tumbled into homelessness. Policymakers cluelessly, and I'd say cruelly, removed what little sustenance families could count on under AFDC (Aid for Families with Dependent Children). The replacement, Temporary Assistance for Needy Families (TANF), brought forth the tough-love approach so "needy" families would yank their bootstraps and leave poverty behind. Single mothers were expected to be grateful for those benevolent, but temporary, crumbs from the rich man's table even though they contributed mightily to soaring family homelessness. Dismazing.

My opportunity to improve federal homelessness policy happened in March, 2011. My congresswoman, Judy Biggert, invited me to screen our documentary, *on the edge: Family Homelessness in America,* to Members of Congress, staff and a slew of agency representatives. My friend and film guru Laura Vazquez and I felt our hard work might pay off.

Laura and I relished the opportunity to screen our documentary to such an influential audience. The Secretary of HUD at the time, Shawn Donovan, attended. Our dream was for all 435 Members of Congress, staffers and all federal agency staff to hear the heartbreaking stories of the seven courageous women in our film. But that didn't happen. Those in the audience, a meager representation of those who should have been there, evidently didn't get the message.

Our documentary, released in 2010, won several awards, including the Big Muddy Film Festival and the Broadcast Education Association's Best of Festival honors. In 2012, *on the edge* was shown on PBS stations across the nation over Mother's Day weekend. It's a classic. Still true more than 10 years after its release.

We had another huge moment when our film was screened at the Naperville Film Festival in September 2011. I was shocked seeing a full theater. Three hundred or so individuals chose to see our film. It was thrilling! The op-ed piece I wrote to thank the event organizers reflects my state of mind at a time that seems like a million years ago:

With what seems to be a growing discord about the need to help families and individuals struggling for survival, the crowd at this film was on the far opposite end of the spectrum. My challenge urging them to participate in a "compassion epidemic" brought cheers instead of jeers. This positive energy gives a huge boost to those of us engaged in helping stave off the devastation of homelessness. My Naperville-based nonprofit organization, HEAR US Inc., continues to give voice and visibility to homeless children and youth through projects like *on the edge*.

Little did I know that in November 2005 when I left the Naperville border heading out on my unconventional sojourn—to chronicle faces and voices of homeless kids from across the nation for **My Own Four Walls**—that I'd be heading out for my 7*th* cross-country trip and our country would be in an economic quagmire that makes previous times of trouble pale. With the child poverty rate at a record high 22%, dark clouds loom on the horizon, especially for homeless families with toddlers, the subject of our new film, *Littlest Nomads*.

Hard to think about times that now, in 2020, seem like the good ol' days. I've met wonderful people in my travels who helped me keep my sense of direction. Knowing I filmed and produced such a high caliber film, viewed by hundreds of thousands of people across the world, renews my sense of purpose during those moments when I feel "lost."

Three Generations Lost

Saundra, her daughter, Sandra, and her 13-year old granddaughter, Sonya, lived in a central valley Oregon city. Saundra agreed to let me interview them in September, 2019. The school district's homeless liaison arranged for us to meet at her office. A well-appointed space with full bathroom and laundry, these two offerings were appreciated by those of us living a nomadic existence. I could hear the three engaged in family chatter as they took turns using the shower. They relished the relatively luxurious bathroom amenities—clean towels, hotel soap and shampoo—as much as they appreciated the opportunity for a hot shower.

When they emerged, they waited in the kitchenette. The liaison made sure they had plenty of snacks and drinks. I interviewed them separately in an adjacent room. Saundra settled into a comfy chair and let loose the excruciating tale of her fall into homelessness. It started when the modest duplex she lived in was sold and the new owners raised the rent. She tried finding a place that would take her Section 8 housing voucher. She ended up living in a small car for several months with her then 11-year-old granddaughter, two dogs and a cat. Sonya's mother lived elsewhere. Sandra dealt with multiple problems that made it impossible for her to fulfill her parental responsibilities.

Because they had moved out of the duplex before the eviction could be served, Saundra didn't lose her housing certificate. A landlord agreed to rent to her. They let her move in. Then came a snafu with one of the utility companies that claimed she owed more than she thought. Local agencies offered limited help—not enough to take care of utilities. So, they went back to the streets. This time Saundra moved into a bedraggled, mold-filled old

RV. It sat in a parking lot ignored by city code inspectors. Her granddaughter moved in with a friend.

Saundra's story followed the now-familiar pattern of other struggling families. Her unexpected responsibility of raising a grandchild was daunting enough. Add to it the need to find a place that would take a housing voucher coupled with the cost of utility security deposits and past due balances, battling collection agencies, stress, and health crisis. Homelessness again was inevitable.

I interviewed Sonya, the granddaughter. She shared the logistical side of their experiences—how hot it was in the car during summer months, how hard it was to sleep in their crowded car, and the joy of being able to shower at a friend's house. She got ready for school in the jam-packed car. She recognized that some people were scary. She fretted their highly-mobile existence. She observed that her grandmother "needs a lot of help, and there's nobody helping her."

The dogs became collateral damage—one dog got away as they were trying to straighten out their belongings in the car. They never found him. The other also ran away and was picked up by the pound. It would have taken $1,000 to get him back.

School offered free lunch: a plus. Sonya's close friends learned of her plight. She was bullied by others. She managed to keep her grades up. She was able to participate in school activities, like field trips. She astutely recognized that she wasn't the only kid in this situation. And she demolished the stereotypes of homelessness, saying "Just because we're homeless, it doesn't mean we're dirty, gross, and gonna steal from you."

I suspect this family didn't have a lot going for them before homelessness hit. Still, they were doing the best they could. Did they make the best decisions? Probably not. But who does? They had no room for error. Once they fell off track, they had no way to get back on. It takes money. It takes landlords who can overlook flaws in a family's rental history. It takes resources to wipe out past utility arrearages. It takes guidance from someone with the family's best interest at heart.

No. They were lost, and I'd be surprised if they got back to whatever could be considered normal.

Lost and Tossed

Many women I've met over the years, "got lost" as children when a man shattered their self-worth by sexually abusing them. From all I've read and heard, the impact of such intrusion causes physical and mental trauma that can last a lifetime. It's enough to cause total dysfunction. Trauma also triggers major physical health issues. While everyone around them gets on with their lives, women who have been abused can feel like aliens in their bodies, families and communities.

In January 2007, the homeless liaison in the Lafayette, Louisiana, school district contacted me about Angela. Angela was the director of a family shelter in nearby Opelousas, a small city north of Lafayette. If I hadn't been given the low-down on Angela's life, I would have figured she was "just" a dedicated family shelter director.

Without any hesitancy, Angela shared that she and her nine children stayed at the shelter a few years earlier. Her journey from homelessness to running the shelter didn't seem like a big deal to her. Running a household with nine kids prepared her for the challenge of running a family shelter with dozens of families.

I spent a week with her. She showed me around town. She introduced me to staff and shelter residents, and made sure I met people in her life who have supported the shelter and more. I sat in on staff and resident meetings, in awe of Angela's astute way of handling people.

The second time I met her was in 2008 when Laura Vazquez and I spent a week at the shelter to interview mothers for our film on family homelessness. Angela welcomed us and eased our path into the shelter, letting the women know they could trust us with their stories. Angela mentioned she had a story to tell, and from what I knew of her, she'd make a good interview.

Laura and I worked nicely together. Her vast professionalism and skillful documentary talents balanced well with my extensive yet down to earth knowledge of family homelessness. Laura did the interviews. I handled the camera. She taught me a lot about filmmaking. Those techniques have come in handy over the years. I clipped the mic on Angela's lapel and we headed down the road of her story.

Sometimes you know where you're headed. Sometimes your destination surprises you. Angela took us through her life. She wasn't embarrassed by her years of poverty, her choice of mates, or the bumps on her road. She was understandably proud of her move from shelter resident to director, a transition that reflected her hard work and competence. Before moving to the top position, she had shown her worth by preparing meals for the shelter residents. Her desire to give back to the place that saved her and her kids from homelessness was immeasurable. Sister Anne Byrne, a Roman Catholic nun who was an earlier shelter director, mentored Angela.

They remained friends until Sister Anne's death in 2017.

As compelling as Angela's story was, Laura and I both felt it was missing a piece. The morning as we prepared to leave, Angela revealed the part of her life she'd kept secret.

When she was a child, her mother's boyfriend sexually abused her on a regular basis. A traumatic experience, she told her closest friend who urged her to tell her mother. Angela did, but "She didn't believe me. She did nothing…when I think of it, home was really not home…I feel that she chose him over me."

Countless times, I've heard of a mother choosing her boyfriend over the well-being of her child. All I can say is, "it's complicated." Most often, it has to do with what the mother had experienced in her lifetime. Abuse. Trauma. These events cloud the person's thinking. Sometimes the mother and daughter work it out. Sometimes not. For Angela and her mother, it took years.

Angela ended up moving to her grandparents' home. Her grandmother believed her.

I often get asked why women who are homeless have so many kids. I can point out the obvious. They weren't homeless when they had their children. This wasn't a career plan. Birth control is hard to come by. It's complicated. No matter what I say, some fail to grasp what's behind the family size issue.

But Angela figured out why she chose to have a large family. "That is why the things in my life happened the way they did. I was looking for something to replace that empty spot that I felt from not having the security of a home…I think that's why I got pregnant. I got married. Had the kids. You know, I thought that if I had all those things, I'd be happy. If my mom would have just listened, and believed what I was telling her, we would be much closer."

I've seen Angela a few times since that interview. She had to give up her dream job running the shelter because of serious health problems—the kind that often accompany the experiences of trauma she endured. She worked at a variety of jobs, but ended up on disability because of her poor health. Still, lots of good stuff happened for her. She met Martin. Fell in love. They bought a double-wide trailer she lives in to this day. Martin died tragically and way too soon. But Angela is a survivor of tough circumstances. She's held it together.

When I visited with her in 2020, we rehashed her journey. She's the proud grandmother of 17. Her children, all grown, are doing well. Most have made their way through college and are contributing to the world. Angela and her mother reconciled not long ago.

Somehow, with an inner GPS and good people to guide her along the way, Angela found her way. She's enriched my life. She made me glad I entered the little town of Opelousas.

Laura and I interviewed others on that trip in 2008. Tonya, one of the women we interviewed during our visit there, passed away in 2017. She struggled so hard against the forces of addiction, and relied on the safe structure of the shelter. In such a vulnerable condition, it's not surprising that Tonya and others stumble. It's our loss when that happens.

You can watch *on the edge* by visiting the HEAR US website, hearus.us.

Lost in the Oregon Woods

As a long-time camper, I have a pretty good idea what the hardships of tent camping include. But I have no idea what it entails with kids involved. I got a glimpse in October 2007. I was in Oregon for a national conference for homeless liaisons.

I connected with a school district homeless liaison in McMinnville, a mid-size city about an hour southwest of Portland. She was helping a family—mom, boyfriend, and three young girls. They were living in the woods, in a tent, on a church's property. The liaison and I met early in one morning and headed out to the woods. The family agreed to let me hang with them a few days.

The forecast threatened rain. I was happy when it didn't. The temps were in the mid-30s and I had my camera gear. We first greeted Michael. He came out of the tent while Gina helped her girls finish getting ready for school. I could hear them—brushing hair, finding jackets, getting the kittens out of the way.

Their dome tent was one of the larger ones. They got it for $50, on sale from Walmart. They had a little propane stove running, providing a risky level of welcome heat. They were the only campers left in what was previously a small encampment on the edge of church property. They landed here in May, with no options.

Their tenting area abutted a municipal park. The girls and mom walked to the park bathroom, about a block away, to finish getting cleaned up. Then Michael walked them to the bus stop. We made plans to connect later at the library.

After school I met with the girls and Michael. The kids got to work on the computers. Gina, who was there for another appointment, joined us.

They told me their plans. They needed to hit the grocery store and find a can of propane for their stove. We walked to the local bus stop and hopped on. I couldn't help but be impressed by the sense of camaraderie between the bus riders and driver.

At the store, Michael headed to find propane. I stayed with Gina and her sweet but rambunctious girls who considered grocery shopping entertainment. Gina's challenge? Figure out what foods she could afford that she could easily cook on their little propane stove.

As they shopped, the girls saw their classmates and waved. It was a challenge to keep track of the threesome. Rose, the youngest, 5-ish, was super hyper. Crystal, the middle girl, about 9-years-old, wandered off in her own little world. The oldest, 12-year-old Angelina, tried to act cool. Gina's struggles with controlling the girls became evident and painful to watch as this expedition continued. The checkout line, with the standard tempting candy display, was the finale. Gina let the girls each pick out their favorite.

Mike returned with propane. He could focus on tasks at hand. The bigger problem of how they would move from camping to housing seemed beyond him.

He and Gina told me about the difficulties of getting a housing authority voucher. They felt like they had to hide their relationship from the Department of Human Services. With the 1996 changes in welfare policies, few two-parent households qualified for assistance. Households with unmarried couples were even less likely to get help. Yeah, I get the theory. But the reality complicates things. Michael had a scheme that involved he and Gina getting married. She wasn't too hot on that idea.

So, poor Gina, who had a grueling day with interviews and other stuff, went "home" to cook pork chops on their little stove. She had one pan, limited propane and no food prep space. She navigated a cramped tent, with three hyper kids, two kittens, and Michael. The monsoon-like Oregon November weather kept everyone inside.

No TV, no electricity, no running water, no privacy. The park bathroom, when open, required a creepy walk through the woods, down a winding, treacherous path. Angelina and Michael headed off in the rain to wash dishes. My hackles were raised, worried about the nefarious possibilities of that arrangement.

The other reality? Critters. A rat had gotten into their not-well-secured metal cooler. The one they kept right outside their tent to store food. When they found the rat, it was dead. And stinky. Michael took care of the disposal task. Gina kept things fairly organized in the tent, a challenge because they had nowhere for stuff. Having rats or other critters in the tent was a constant hazard.

I couldn't help but think about the strategy of camping for this family. Laundry was an expensive logistical challenge. I could understand why they'd have hygiene issues, with no hot shower. Privacy, other than their location being out of sight, was impossible in that small tent. When one (or more) of them got sick, what happened then? No car to hop into to get to the clinic. Grocery shopping, as I witnessed, was a grueling task, and required money that they did not have. Cooking and cleaning would challenge the most capable homemaker. And the kids? How did they do homework?

How many families endure these kinds of living conditions? At least this family had tremendous support from their homeless liaison. Without her, they would be totally lost. Stuck in a tent in the woods, dealing with rats, rain and relentless cold winds. I couldn't help but wonder what lessons Gina's girls would remember from their months of camping.

After I left the area, I got word that Gina and the girls got a place through the housing authority. After six months in a tent, that had to be a relief. But the relief also brought the challenge of moving from what I would describe as a feral lifestyle to civilization. They crawled out of the woods into an apartment.

I know from my camping days how easy it is to get a little messy. And that was for me, for a week, without kids. Evidently, they had issues keeping their new housing in proper order. It was an adjustment that needed to be made or they'd lose their home. If they lost that opportunity, they would be lost for sure.

Idaho Strong, But Lost

Dads are stereotypically the family breadwinner. The homeless liaison in Nampa, Idaho introduced me to Byron, a strong looking dad who cried openly in front of me. He, his infirm wife and their four kids were "camping" in the backyard of a friend's house on the outskirts of town.

They became homeless when property owner of the home where they'd lived for more than five years told them to get out. He was selling the place. Unable to find another home they could afford, the family retreated to a small camper and makeshift accommodations. Their hardscrabble campsite reflected the desperate and destitute reality that homelessness brought.

Nampa, a mid-size city in western Idaho, was Byron's hometown. He and his family returned when he needed to care for his ailing mother. She later died. They settled there. They lived their version of normal until the eviction. That changed everything. It provided challenges for this devoted dad that tested his fortitude.

During the interview, Angie, his wife of over 20 years, sat in the small, dark, cramped camper, surrounded by her beloved dogs and cat. A botched bariatric surgery left her unable to eat most foods. Byron told me she was dying of malnutrition.

Byron and Angie also had a severely disabled son who suffered a brain hemorrhage when he was born. Byron described their son's situation, "He lost 80% of the front left lobe of his brain. He's 15, a little over 6 foot, 250 (lbs.), and functions at the level of a five-year-old."

Complaints from neighbors about the family's camping area spurred the authorities to threaten them. When I met the family, they had just days to move on. Where? They didn't know.

To earn money, Byron did serious scrapping. He filled his pickup truck bed with metal. They had a washer and dryer, but it was in storage, so he spent $100 a week doing laundry. As he described his efforts to find more suitable housing arrangements, he underscored the insane gauntlet for income-challenged families. Leasing application fees for the adults, anyone over 18, would set this family back $200 each time. Moving required pet deposits adding hundreds more to the process. Untenable.

The worst was his description of their hopeless situation. They didn't qualify for any state assistance. Getting their kids to school every day was close to impossible. It would be more so when they pulled up stakes. "Now I have to play hide-me from the state so they don't take my kids, especially my special-needs child," he said, voice breaking. "You want to destroy me? Take him…" and he turned away and walked a few steps to regain his composure, giving me time to regain mine.

This family was lost, not because they took a wrong turn. They were upended by the economics of housing and the lack of options. Their previously normal, stable existence shattered. Their makeshift shelter reflected their deteriorating situation. As much as Byron tried to hold things together, he couldn't. I'm not sure who could have. I know I couldn't.

Being Lost — 'Our Worst Fear'

Our family lived in Sarasota, Florida for a few years when I was 6 – 8-years-old. It's where I got my first camera, a Brownie. I started taking pictures then. Now I have tens of thousands of photos, filled with memories. I've been back to this vacation mecca several times as I've traveled across the Sunshine State. I'm dismazed at the affluence, and poverty.

I toured Florida in 2016 seeking stories for a film project I was hired to do for the Institute of Children, Poverty, and Homelessness (ICPH). No shortage of possibilities. I could drive through most motel parking lots and find families down on their luck in that unforgiving economy.

What happened to the Florida where I grew up as a kid? Today's Florida seems exceptionally tough. More than 20% of

Florida's children live in poverty. The largest group is African-American. The numbers of students identified as homeless shot up as a result of multiple devastating storms. It now approaches the 100,000 mark, not including babies and toddlers.

Hoity-toity Sarasota has a crisis of family homelessness. They have for some time, to no surprise. Few family shelters. Scarce subsidized housing. The cost of housing is off the charts. The average rent for a 3-bedroom apartment in Sarasota County is over $1,300. It seems that Sarasota's tight-fisted approach to family homelessness was to repel those in need by making help hard to find. From what I've read and from conversations with local advocates, some community leaders want to avoid attracting families from other, less-affluent areas.

I met Christina and two of her daughters at a school resource center in Sarasota. She, her husband, their four kids and a dog previously enjoyed life in this delightful area. Her husband worked until a back injury and subsequent surgery knocked the family out of their 2,400 sq. ft. home with a pool. They doubled up with relatives in a seniors-only development. That imperiled the host family, creating a tremendous amount of stress. Christina and her family periodically spent a few days at a cheap motel to alleviate the overcrowding. She found a minimum-wage, part-time job to make ends meet.

Christina shared with me her worst worries. Lack of privacy was agonizing. The chaos and tensions made life hard for all under that too-small roof. Not being able to have birthday parties for her kids hurt a lot, too. Their stuff sat on a porch before they were able to put it in storage, so much of it got ruined. Her worst fears? Losing custody of her kids. Realizing their marriage was in shambles.

Finding a place to live was proving to be impossible. Christina would call a rental listing and be rejected because she was getting outside assistance. She said the property managers, "didn't want to take help from an agency because they [the prospective landlord] thought I'm not going to pay my rent if I needed help to move in somewhere."

When you are that lost, how do you get back on track?

The best protection any woman
can have... is courage.

- Elizabeth Cady Stanton

CHAPTER 10
Stranger Danger

In the mid-1980s, I was responsible for media relations at Joliet Catholic Charities. I knew nothing about what I was doing. What I learned was helpful in dealing with the media madness we experienced as our "Charlie's Bill" campaign got underway in 1993. In my Project REACH days (2003 - 2005), I was able to lure media coverage to counteract the unenlightened school districts that kept homeless kids out of school. Those experiences taught me what I needed to know to attract media coverage and make HEAR US work.

When I kicked off my HEAR US venture in Fall of 2005, the uniqueness of my HEAR US endeavor received a good amount of coverage. Mostly, the stories—woman sells all she owns and hits the road in an RV and drives all over the country to help homeless kids—oozed Mother Teresa-type adulation. I'm far from Mother Teresa. But I didn't argue because I knew stories like this would capture attention and hopefully support. This was before social media, so all I could do was share the stories through our e-newsletter and post them on the HEAR US website.

The ripple effect of this initial coverage was that the Chicago area media was aware of, and interested in, my unconventional endeavor. It helped that I had a relationship with many area journalists. Media interest was still warm when I returned from my first round of travel in the summer of 2006.

When Mark Saxenmeyer, a reporter for the Chicago Fox TV news station contacted me in September 2006, I welcomed the opportunity for him to do a story.

He came out to the western suburbs where I holed up before hitting the road again. I made sure my rig, Tillie1, was presentable, inside and out. In addition to the interview, he wanted me to drive while he and the camera guy rode along. When you spend that much time—a couple hours at least—with professionals looking for a story, lots of chatting goes on.

Mark is the perfect guy for a job in the news world. He and I ended up in a conversation that surprised me at the time. He asked me, off-camera, if I was scared. Before I had a chance to answer, he gave me his reason why I should be. Plenty of scary people lurk out there. I could tell he was concerned for my safety, something I gave minimal worry to most of the time.

Well, yeah, I knew sometimes my circumstances would land me in places that could be dangerous. But I knew and still know that not everyone out there is scary. The people I used to think were scary—like some of the guys at the shelters I ran—were not. On the other hand, individuals I knew who held positions of public trust, were. I discovered the scary ones from personal experience. I chose to hang onto the thought that not everyone I met would be scary. I fell back on my street sense. Relax, Mark, but thanks for caring!

Scary Stuff Out There

The prospect of backroads travel frightens many people I've talked to on my journey. I'm not sure what they're afraid of. Or maybe I am. Could it be poverty and race? For those who have never done much traveling, going outside their comfort zone creates fear. For others, like my friend Gary, they have another perspective.

Gary, an imposing Black man, oversees the emergency shelter in the university town of DeKalb, Illinois. I hung out at that shelter while working with Laura on my video projects. As Gary and I chatted one day, he told me he couldn't do what I was doing. *Why not?*

His reasoning made dismazing sense. A person of color—male or female—traveling alone on the backroads all over the country? Crazy-dangerous. His Black-self made him a target. That was a perspective I hadn't considered. Even more so than for a white woman traveling solo, he was right. Racism would add significant risk. In the areas in the South that I'd seen, their Confederate flags flying even from fire stations, a person could disappear without a trace. Scary for Gary. Eye-opening for me.

June 2020. Our nation's struggle with police murders of Black men and women has exploded. Since the appalling arrest and murder of George Floyd in Minneapolis, we have seen what seems like endless other atrocious encounters between cops and Black men and women. The stories of violence experienced by people of color give chilling validation to Gary's concerns. Countless, and largely unreported, incidents of racial inequity also have a major impact on education. Another topic for another book written by someone better qualified than me.

Alone, On My Own

From my first year on the road, I'd been totally alone in some campgrounds. I've traveled year-round, much of it not in the normal camping months. I've searched for places that would be open: hopefully with electricity. My preference has always been public campgrounds. They tend to offer more space, places to hike or at least sit by the water, and they need to be supported in my "use them or lose them" way of thinking.

As nonchalant as I appear to be when I park and plug-in at these remote places, I have that niggling thought of the "boogey man." For that reason, I eschew scary novels and movies. But still….

Months after Hurricane Katrina, I encountered my first scary public campground. It was my first year traveling in southern Louisiana. In those days, I relied on my trusty but imperfect atlas to find campgrounds. Looking for a place to stay, if I saw a state park with a tent symbol on the map, I headed toward it. What wasn't obvious to me was the type of road—often bone-jarring gravel—between me and my place of rest.

My friends tell me I have a high pain tolerance. That's good and bad. As I headed to the state park that day, I'd say my tolerance was a liability. The horrendously long stretch of road rattled everything in my little house on wheels. I felt like the panels would fall off and my fillings would fall out. But I kept going. It was the only campground anywhere near me. And because that's what I tend to do in tough situations—keep going.

When I finally arrived at the Tickfaw State Park office I was relieved and awed. It was by far the most remote place I'd ever camped. I requested a campsite with electricity for the night. No.

No? The ranger said FEMA had reserved all the campsites.

Are they all occupied? No.

May I have one? No.

Why not? FEMA rules.

By this time, early on, FEMA had gotten on my nerves. I had interviewed families that had endless difficulties with FEMA. This federal agency whose sole purpose was to assist Americans in need of help during emergencies was a bungling bureaucratic mess. And now they were keeping me from plugging in and getting a decent night's sleep.

I was able to beg for a tent, non-electric site. That was my only choice because driving back on that treacherous road, in the dark, was not an option. From what I could see, NONE of the electric campsites were occupied. And the tent sites had just a few campers.

Since my RV was self-contained, I had no need to step outside. Looking out my front window, I saw a scruffy-looking guy walking through the park. My imagination went wild. I had read enough stories of bands of houseless people wandering through neighborhoods in New Orleans and Baton Rouge. I created my own fear-based drama. I pictured having my rig stolen by people desperate for a place to live. I envisioned my body tossed in a near-by swamp. What compounded my issue? Cell coverage was spotty and calling for help uncertain. Sometimes I'm my own worst enemy.

Options, Free If I Stealth It

With a vehicle of either Tillie's size, the options for overnight parking outside of campgrounds were and are limited. My fallback? "Camp Walmart." With stores all over the country, Walmart allows RVers to park in their spacious lots so they might shop in their cavernous stores. That policy has changed over the years. Some Walmarts ban "camping" because too many people turned to the nation's #1 retailer for living space because of homelessness. But I frequent their lots any time I can. No electricity, but free.

State parks or government campgrounds are my preference. They charge. Often not cheap ($30+). I am too frugal. But sometimes I need them for water, electricity, showers and waste disposal. Private campgrounds are my least favorite, typically with no space between lots and they cost more. But if I have to, I will.

I rarely sleep on the street. Many municipalities ban sleeping in vehicles. The last thing I want, once I hit the sack, is someone disturbing me. I have worked on perfecting my "stealth" mode over the years. I make sure my windows are covered so no one knows if anyone is inside.

In early 2012, I was invited to screen *on the edge: Family Homelessness in America* at Pomona College in Claremont, CA. How exciting to be invited to that prestigious institution located in an affluent part of the city! Parking lots are often not RV-friendly and this was no exception. So, I parked on a nearby street and made my way into the school.

The event went well. Respectable crowd. Vibrant discussion following our gut-wrenching documentary. I was bone-tired when we finished. I made my way out to Tillie1. No ticket. A good sign! My tired brain talked me into staying on that city street, in that non-threatening neighborhood for the night. I would leave early before people noticed me. I crawled into bed and died on the pillow.

At some point in the wee morning hours, I was awakened from my dead sleep by thumping outside. Right above me! Yikes! Someone was climbing up the ladder outside, above my head at the back of my rig. The invader clomped up onto the roof. What?? With my deepest and scariest voice, I bellowed, "Get off of there!"

It worked. I heard the prowler scamper down the ladder. Phew! The next thing I heard was, "But I like homeless kids." I attributed the tone to an inebriated-sounding male college student. He was evidently sober enough to read the signage on the back of my vehicle. That was scary-weird, but no harm done.

Hell No, Sheriff Joe!

In 2013, my friend Pat LaMarche and I headed out on our longest joint trip. We spent six weeks touring along the fabled Route 66. We headed westward: all the way to California. Along the route we attended events, hosted by local activists who were happy to use us to call attention to homelessness. We wrapped up that overly-ambitious tour in Los Angeles with a great interview on the cable news program, *The Young Turks*. There our twosome was immortalized as the *Babes of Wrath* after Steinbeck's *Grapes of Wrath*. We then headed toward Phoenix, AZ, where a friend offered a spot to park.

Pat, a professional and audacious journalist who always looked for stories that needed to be told, wanted to interview Sheriff Joe Arpaio. At the time, he was the infamous chief lawman of Maricopa County where Phoenix is located. His reputation as a media-savvy, race-baiting, minority-hating, chain-gang loving enforcer of whatever laws he chose made him a natural target for Pat. At the time Pat was writing for Huffington Post. I scoffed at her suggestion. I told her that he wouldn't give her the time of day. That never stopped her. She called and talked to one of his people. Amazingly enough, she was granted an interview. We made tracks to Phoenix with new purpose.

No way in hell I was letting her go in there without me. So, I grabbed my camera. My new job was to chronicle this momentous occasion on film. We entered the Wells Fargo building in downtown Phoenix and went up to the 19th floor where this unconventional lawman had his shrine-like office. As we waited, we could hear a conversation between Sheriff Joe and his assistant who arranged the interview.

Sheriff: "Where is she from?"

Assistant replied, "Huffington Post."

Sheriff bellowed, "What? Huffington Post? They hate me!" Then the brave sheriff showed his true courage, "I'm not going in there alone. Where's a deputy? Get me a deputy."

An officer quickly appeared and was instructed to protect the sheriff. "You. You're coming in with me."

I was gobsmacked that the Sheriff actually came in and allowed Pat to interview him. I was equally surprised he didn't stop me from filming the process.

I'd doubt the Pope would have an office decked out in such a self-aggrandizing way. Every media story, magazine cover, award, honorary degree, and campaign poster that featured his name and face was framed and hung in his office. I gawked as Pat interviewed him. When she finished, she bragged me up as she tends to do. Pat told this infamous lawman about me living in a van, interviewing homeless kids, etc.

His response, as he was autographing the full-color poster of himself, was "Are you packing?"

Huh? Packing?

It took a moment for me to catch on. He was asking if I was armed.

Um, no, I replied, dismissing the concept with an eye-rolling shake of my head.

No? He was flabbergasted! *No?*

"No. I used to run one of the largest homeless shelters in Illinois and I didn't need to carry then, and I don't need to carry now," I said, disarming this fear-baiting lawman. He was still flabbergasted as we made our way out of his palace back to the real world. His poster would never see the light of day until Pat hung it over the toilet in her house.

Annie, Get Your Gun!

My closest call with guns was in October 2016 after what had been a grueling national homelessness conference in Orlando, Florida. I had stealth-camped in Tillie2, parked behind the conference hotel. My friends and I were fighting for the survival of an organization undergoing upheaval. I spent very little time in my rig. I crept out there at night. Hit the sack. I went back inside the hotel each day.

Hotels don't like people sleeping in their parking lots. I stayed stealthy. It was hot at night but I didn't want to blow my cover. I cracked open the roof vents just enough to let a little air in. When the conference ended, I bolted out of the city as fast as I could. I headed toward Horseshoe Beach to seek refuge at a tiny, cheap campground right on the Gulf of Mexico.

When I arrived, I was delighted. No other campers were there. The gravel lot on the edge of the Gulf had minimal features: just electricity and proximity to the healing sound of waves rolling in. I backed up my van to the water's edge. I opened the back doors and breathed a sigh of relief. I had plenty to process after our brutal loss at the conference. Sun, fresh air and water were just what I needed. This municipal campground had an unusual way of collecting fees. A woman went around with her clipboard and money box to register campers. But no one came. So, I just settled in and relaxed. I figured I could safely leave my back doors open. I had a screen to keep out the flying critters. The open air made up for the stealth hell in Orlando.

That night, I was in bed, reading. I heard the crunch of gravel as a car pulled into the lot. *Shit*, my tired self thought. *Something to worry about.* Car door slammed. Footsteps. "Hello…" hollered a woman's voice. I relaxed a bit when she shouted that she had come to collect the $20 fee. I had the cash next to my bed so I didn't even get up. I spoke to her over my shoulder as she stood at the back opening.

All of sudden, clunk, metal hit the ground. She gasped. Bent over. She muttered that she had just dropped her gun. Alrighty! And it didn't go off, to my delight. I handed her my money and counted my blessings that my closest gun incident ended peacefully.

Danger Within, Part 1

When Laura Vazquez and I embarked on our film project, *on the edge: Family Homelessness in America*, I learned what it took to make a genuine documentary. In addition to filming interviews of women and youth, she insisted we go for the contrary individuals, those whose opinions or positions about family homelessness did not jive with ours.

My #1 suggestion was Phil Mangano. At the time he was the head of the U.S. Interagency Council on Homelessness. I had followed stories about him. I considered him astoundingly ignorant about the issues facing families and youth.

I looked into his schedule and found that he'd be in Springfield, Illinois in July 2008, a perfect time for a road trip for the two of us! We made an appointment to interview him and headed to Springfield, where I had spent plenty of time lobbying at the Capitol for homeless kids' and adults' issues.

Laura and I strategized the opportunity. We encountered one delay. He had a scheduling problem. But then we got our chance. My *invisible homeless kids* blog says it best.

4/30/09 invisible homeless kids

But the clincher was last summer when my video partner, Laura Vazquez, and I tried to interview him [Mangano] for our documentary about homeless families. This pre-arranged interview was in Springfield, Illinois.

*We shared our purpose and questions,
so as not to "Michael Moore" him.*

*And, after he blew off our
morning appointment, we had to
follow him around all day. Finally, 13
hours after our initial time, having
listened to far more Phil Mangano
than I would ever choose, we got him
for a few minutes. As I put on his mic,
once he sat down, he said,* I sure hope
you're not going to ask me about those
kids... *or something very close to that.*

Laura assured him that, yes, Mr.
Mangano, that's exactly what we're
here for, just as we had told your
'people' as we arranged this.

*The interview, as I remember, was
just a waste of time.*

*Me, I seethed as I stood behind
the camera that was too expensive to
toss his way. I couldn't quite control
myself when, after the interview, he
made a remark that insinuated that
communities wanting to serve
homeless families and teens could do
so if they chose. I disagreed, knowing
a bit how HUD funds programs, or
not, depending on compliance with*

*policies and priorities, stated and
implied.*

*Then Laura disagreed with a
remark he made about statistics.
Between the two of us, we probably
ruined his night. He stormed off,
shouting at us as he crossed the hall to
leave. We stood there, not really
knowing what to make about the show
of anger that far exceeded a typical
disagreement.*

The interview validated what I had heard and read. I've had
a few encounters with scary people like this. They're usually the
ones with the power to do something constructive about policies
and practices to alleviate homelessness. Something's going on with
them that creates this destructive hostility. Anger issues?
Experiences of trauma? Dispassionate indifference? Sadism?

My scary stuff pales in comparison to those who deal with
it under their own roof. Scary has a different look when it's a matter
of life and death, as it is for so many vulnerable families and
individuals.

Danger Within, Part 2

Other than the handful of elected officials who have
experienced homelessness, few have tried to learn about the issue
that affects millions of their constituents. Pat LaMarche and I, aka
the Babes of Wrath, constantly tried to devise ways of raising
awareness of homelessness.

I had been filming in Oregon, Washington and Idaho, and
had picked up Pat in Missoula, Montana. We created the Babes of

Wrath "Homeless on the Range" trip. Our route included Montana's Blackfoot Nation, North Dakota's oil fields, and South Dakota's Standing Rock protest of the Dakota Access Pipeline. We explored issues that concerned us. Including, the efforts of Native Americans to grapple with abject poverty on their Montana reservation.

We witnessed the greedy fracking operations in oil-rich North Dakota. We joined protestors at Standing Rock in South Dakota, where Pat interviewed and I filmed this iconic effort.

We then headed to Illinois for the much-awaited George Winston benefit concert for HEAR US in Naperville on Oct. 13, 2016. On the backroads en route to Illinois, the Babes of Wrath concocted a scheme to help then-Speaker of the House Paul Ryan get a clue about how significant homelessness was. We were almost arrested.

As we rumbled along the backroads of Wisconsin, I pondered the stack of bumper stickers we had that proclaimed "LOVE: Make America Kind Again." How could we use these bumper stickers in a worthwhile way? Hmmmm… Knowing we were going near Janesville, Wisconsin, a location of one of Paul Ryan's district offices, our brains got thinking. We could sticker-bomb the area outside his office! This wouldn't be doing any harm. And who knows? It might do good.

That evening, we scouted the area around the Speaker's office, a storefront in bucolic downtown Janesville. I had been there before when I dropped off materials about my HEAR US work. The area was deserted, so we scampered outside his office and slapped our bumper stickers as many places as we could—lightposts, park benches, trash cans. We then scooted.

Excited about the possibilities, we camped at the local Camp Walmart. The next day we headed over to his office super early. I wanted a good parking spot across from his office. Pat made a cardboard sign asking for help for the homeless. She planted herself on the sidewalk right outside Mr. Ryan's office, exercising her 1st Amendment rights. I sat in T2 across the street. Ready with my video camera, I knew this could be, um, interesting. A middle-aged woman dropped a few bucks into Pat's cup. A group of teens stopped to thank her for calling attention to homelessness and added coins to her cup. A few of them said they were homeless, too.

It didn't take long for those feel-good moments to end. A store owner from the building where the Congressman's office was located, came out to stomp on Pat's 1st Amendment rights. He told her she needed to leave because she was standing in front of the Congressman's office. She assured him she knew that. He threatened to call the police. Pat, in an incredible display of civility and calm, said she was legally within her bounds and was collecting for homeless kids. That had no positive impact on Mr. Store Owner. He, along with Ryan's staff, called the police. In a heartbeat an officer arrived.

I don't think they have many demonstrations in front of the Speaker's office. When House Speaker Denny Hastert (my congressman before he was thrown in jail for child sexual abuse) had demonstrators at his downtown Batavia, Illinois office, the police kept their distance. But Janesville's finest took a pretty aggressive stand. He charged over to Pat who, by that time, had collected about $6. Mr. Officer didn't appreciate her efforts. I filmed as Pat stood quietly while the officer tried to rattle her cage. I figured I was about to be part of the action when she pointed over to me.

Oops! I dropped the video camera down to my lap. I decided to keep it running to capture the audio. I figured it could get interesting. Mr. Officer strode purposely toward my sinister-looking vehicle, T2, with its darkened windows. When he approached, he asked what I was doing.

Really?

Then he said he'd like to search the van. *No.*

No? No. No warrant, no search.

He asked how he would know if I had a bunch of people with weapons inside. I said that I didn't. The conversation continued pointlessly, with me trying to restrain my smart-ass tongue. He eventually backed off, saying he would keep an eye on us.

Pat, in the meantime, went into Ryan's office and left materials on homeless kids. She politely asked them to have Speaker Ryan call us. She informed them that we have been trying to get him to contact us for years. She came out and we departed, peacefully. We watched as a Wisconsin State Trooper raced to the scene of our non-crime. No speeding for me as we made our way out of the Cheesehead state.

Our reward was a totally enjoyable George Winston concert the next night. After the concert, as tired as we were, we commiserated with George about our upcoming political disaster. Our shared fear? That the worst might befall us.

My Scary Stuff Pales in Comparison

Money is the one thing that keeps many parents (often women) in domestic violence relationships. Because so few resources exist to support victims if/when they leave the abuser, they are trapped like a bug in a spider web. I've met plenty of women who shared their experiences of domestic violence. Most were not on camera for fear of retribution from their ex.

Victims react differently depending on so many factors. Some quickly get out of the relationship. Some bounce back and forth. Most stay until they get the courage to leave. Some stay too long, resulting in death or a lifetime of misery. Years ago, I answered the door late at night at the shelter. I discovered a bloody and broken woman. She'd previously stayed at our shelter. The battered woman knew we'd help her or anyone needing refuge – even though we weren't set up to assist women experiencing domestic violence. I've worked with many women who lost housing because of domestic violence. Most are understandably afraid. Not Julianna.

Courage in the Face of Danger

I encountered Julianna on my first cross-country trip back in 2006 in Tempe, Arizona. I had interviewed her daughter Gabriella for my first film, *My Own Four Walls*. Julianna had already "come out" about her history of domestic violence while working with a local women's group in town. Her determination to be part of our film project far outweighed her fear of her ex. (You can see Julianna in our documentary *on the edge: Family Homelessness in America).*

When she was young, Julianna pursued her life's dream. She joined the U.S. Army. There she met the man of her dreams, also in the Army. That man would, in time, become her nightmare. Shortly after they married Julianna got pregnant. She retired from the military to care for their family. Each time her husband returned from a tour of duty she became pregnant. As their relationship deteriorated, this gregarious mother felt trapped and looked for a way out.

As much as she loved raising her family, Julianna wanted to stop having children. Her husband made it very clear that getting her tubes tied was not an option. He raped her at will. She had no choice but to submit to his violence-fueled demands. She knew that involving the military police in their marital disputes would only come back on her and the kids. Julianna displayed faux patterns of familial bliss. Her life seesawed between excruciating eruptions of her husband's anger and brutality when he was home, and deceptive lulls as he was deployed. She withered as she endured his sexual demands which subsequently resulted in pregnancy until she had four children. Then something snapped.

Her job was her sanctuary. She worked as a teacher's aide in the local grade school. With her bubbly personality and ability to bond with even the hardest-to-love child, she was treasured by her students and colleagues. Few knew of Julianna's alternate reality. One social worker, the district's homeless liaison, sensed something going on. Over time that liaison developed a trusting relationship with the beleaguered mother.

As they spoke of her scarce options, Julianna laid out her two-pronged bottom line: "I don't want my kids to change schools, and I won't go back to him." She knew nothing of the federal McKinney-Vento Act that protected the educational rights of homeless students. The law allows parents to decide which school options are in the best interest of the children. The liaison assured Julianna that her kids could stay in their schools, with help to make it feasible. With that in place, Julianna made her move just as her husband threatened to harm her eldest son. She had taken her husband's beatings, but no way in hell was she going to let him hit any of the children. She ushered the kids out of the house and down the street to a neighbor's house.

Because the local shelter didn't accept older boys (her oldest son was 14 at the time), Julianna couldn't go there. She refused to split up the family. Julianna and her kids endured what so many families in similar situations go through—a succession of nights sleeping on floors and on the couches of friends and acquaintances. Their piles of plastic bags and bins of possessions traveled with them to their bare-bones, temporary accommodations.

Doubled up. At the mercy of their host family. As precarious as their arrangements were, with several moves over the period of their homelessness, her courage brought survival.

Julianna's life did not turn out the way she'd planned. Her extended family couldn't provide the support needed. She lacked financial wherewithal. She didn't have a car. What she did have was a nontraditional support network. Friends and coworkers extended a hand, a floor, a car, and a listening ear.

When Laura and I met up with her in 2008, Julianna and her kids had recently moved into a subsidized apartment. During the filming process she expounded on her dreams. Buy a home. Get a college degree. Become a teacher. I've heard plenty of women share their plans for getting back on their feet. Few expressed it with as much determination as Julianna. I believed her.

Julianna has clawed her way back to self-sufficiency, with remarkable inner strength that needs to be bottled and sold. She and her kids didn't start out homeless. Working parents, middle-class neighborhood, good schools, plenty of friends.

Julianna took her role as mother seriously. She established "Julianna and Company," a family "business" that was focused on rebuilding their lives. She sought and found constructive activities to occupy her kids. She embraced their new phase: a home of their own, bedrooms for the kids, a sense of order and relative control of their lives. She learned to manage a household, pay bills, keep her kids on the right track and more. Friends helped her get a car.

Despite the semblance of normal, the entire family struggled with trauma. Julianna knew they all needed help to get their heads on straight. After what they'd been through, she sought opportunities to get counseling for all of them.

One of the few times I crossed a professional boundary with any of the people I interviewed was when Julianna asked me if

I'd take her and her kids up to the Grand Canyon. I had Tillie1 then. It offered sufficient room for her kids who sprawled out and slept the whole way: a 5-hour drive. We got to the park and saw snow on the ground. The kids awakened, none of them dressed in appropriate snow clothing. That didn't matter. They bolted out of my camper and frolicked like otters in a river. They threw snowballs and chased each other around. None of them noticed the Grand Canyon just a few yards away.

Julianna and I finally convinced them to give this Wonder of the World a bit of their attention. It was a tough sell. Romping in snow won the day. We had dinner, then drove to a nearby motel. I put the family up for the night while I slept in my humble digs. I was happy to have made this field trip possible.

What's Really Scary?

The dangers facing families and youth in vulnerable situations of homelessness are many. Abuse of all kinds is at the top of the list. Being in a homeless situation makes people extremely vulnerable to predators.

Sex trafficking poses a tremendous risk for desperate teens and young adults. Typically, predators befriend their victims. Provide food, a place to stay, and other things to make life seem good. Once the young person is hooked, the predator coerces her/him to offer sex to strangers for pay. Of course, the predator keeps the money, and confines their victim. Sex trafficking can also trap unwitting, distressed adults. The inevitable impact on the victims ranges from trauma to death.

Parents I've interviewed expressed their deep fear of losing custody of their children. They fear fines or jail for abusing or neglecting their children. The children may be removed from the parents and placed into foster care. Once children are removed, parents face tremendous barriers reuniting. Even though, in most states, homelessness is not a reason on its own for removing children, the fear is real. When neglect or abuse can be documented, it is justified.

Health issues run rampant in the homeless population. Accessing medical care for children or adults is hit or mostly miss. Theoretically, children are eligible for health care under Medicaid through Children's Health Insurance Program (CHIP). That program is fraught with red tape and restrictions. Several states have refused to even establish it. Parents also have difficulty getting health care. High mobility adds to the complications of enrolling in a health care system. Considering the wide range of physical and mental health hazards that homeless families face, their lack of health care is dismazing.

Exposure to hazardous environments is another common risk for families experiencing homelessness. "Beggars can't be choosers" means if someone offers a family a place to sleep, even an unsafe setting, they cannot easily refuse. Sleeping in toxic environments—car repair shops, places close to chemicals from nearby factories, garages filled with poisonous substances—has devastating impact on families, especially young children.

What is truly scary is the total disregard our federal government has for families, especially those in doubled up situations like Julianna and Company. The definition of "homeless" that the U.S. Department of Housing and Urban Development (HUD) uses doesn't consider doubled up to be homeless. Therefore, Julianna's family was not eligible for housing assistance. The battle over the definition of homelessness seems endless. But we can't give up.

The U.S. Department of Education's definition of homeless which came from our Charlie's Law, includes families that have lost housing due to hardship regardless of where they land. This difference in definition means that HUD virtually ignores the millions of families and youth experiencing homelessness which the schools have identified. We have proposed legislation that will change this definition. The sad and scary thing is that many in Congress don't see this as important. I know I've expounded on this seemingly obscure concept throughout the book. It's fueled my fire from day one. We are bound and determined to get HUD's definition aligned with the more accurate one used by the Department of Education and others.

Among other things, families not being able to get help when they lose housing puts them in great peril. They are vulnerable to being harmed by strangers (as well as those they know) just because they are desperate for a place to stay. Stranger danger isn't always strangers.

Scary means different things to different people. Certainly, I had some scary episodes. But they were relatively mild compared to what millions of families and youth in precarious situations encounter every day.

Ask yourself, how do you react when you're afraid? What if you lost your safety network and resources? Can you imagine what that would be like?

Those of us with any sort of solid ground beneath us have no clue what scary means.

You are only free when you realize
you belong to no place –
you belong to every place -- no
place at all. The price is high.
The reward is great.

– Maya Angelou

CHAPTER 11
Oh! The Places I've Gone!

The whimsical expressions of *Oh, the Places You'll Go!* by Dr. Seuss celebrate one's unrestrained travel experiences. I have to say my travel, when I ponder the places I've been, pretty well overwhelms me. With the exception of Alaska, I've spent time in each state, and made it a point to crisscross as many backroads as possible.

Sometimes, when I'm driving in my Zen state of mind, I feel the memories of different places wash over me. I'm awed by what I've seen, the inspiring people I've met, and mind-blowing experiences I've had. It's kind of like reliving a delightful meal. It gives me a renewed sense of purpose and the courage to pursue another destination and project.

To a certain extent, I did decide where to go. My scathingly brilliant creation of a worthwhile project has given me, and hopefully audiences and viewers around the world, a look at homelessness rarely seen or acknowledged. I've focused on the homelessness of mostly invisible families. My observations and experiences have given me a strong platform to challenge HUD's distorted way of dealing with families.

My inspiration to do this highly-mobile project came to me at a time when I was pretty bummed. Having been told that my McKinney-Vento Chicagoland area Project REACH was going to be shut down back in 2005, I had to find something worthwhile to work on, fast. Since I knew nothing would make me want to work for someone else again, I pondered the possibilities. I sat in a comfy chair in my beloved townhome and watched the movie *Winged Migration.* As stunningly beautiful and awe-inspiring as the movie is, the scene of the geese in the Grand Canyon area bought me back to a previous trip there. I went when I was in college in the early 1970s.

I hadn't traveled much since then. I took yearly trips, more like decompression retreats, to Minnesota's pristine Boundary Waters to canoe and camp. Shelter running took a lot out of my life. It also gave back in many ways. Being "locked down" for all those years, I shouldn't be surprised that I had wanderlust. One thing led to another in those early months of 2005.

My audacious brainstorm of traveling to various non-urban places across the country and documenting family homelessness just hit me as the thing to do for all kinds of reasons. Family homelessness was—and still is—pretty much an invisible issue. When mentioned by the media, urban areas get all the attention. I knew that documenting kids experiencing homelessness in non-urban areas would make a tremendous difference in school officials' understanding of this obscure issue.

I could have stayed in the Chicago area where I worked all my adult life. I knew plenty of people who worked with homeless families. Still, going hither and yon to uncover families' stories would certainly lift the veil on the issue. Or so I hoped. And I'd get much-needed drive therapy. Re-reading William Least Heat Moon's *Blue Highways* fueled my fire for backroads travel. I wasn't sure about the RV piece, a concept I used to scoff at, but I figured it could work.

For the most part I was glad I made the choices I made. My routes were determined by the events or film projects I had at the time. I enjoyed a lot of flexibility in my choice of roads and stops along the way. The atlas often indicated a scenic route that was not too much of a detour. If I had time, I'd coddiwomple along the way. The beauty I saw as I traversed the backroads offset the dismazing glitches I encountered and the heart-wrenching stories I heard.

A Trip to Move Mountains, and Not

I don't ponder my HEAR US accomplishments often, but when I do, it bolsters my fragile sense of perspective. To the best of my knowledge, I'm the only one doing what I'm doing: chronicling families experiencing homelessness. Sometimes it feels significant; like something that can move mountains. But, when my capacity for sadness is teetering, it feels like not so much.

That's why I deeply appreciated the heartfelt words of my friend of 30 years, Barbara W. James,

> "Never feel alone in this struggle—you're a LEADER, and that CAN feel very lonely at times. But just remember all those who value and use your work every day—they've got your back. And those whom you film will probably never understand what their willingness to bare their souls means to those who are trying to explain homelessness to disinterested school administrators, politicians, and other decision-makers. One 60-second cut of a story is truly worth thousands of words!!! Remember what happened in Donna [a small Texas town on the Mexican border] as a result of your work? That was amazing!!!"

Barbara led the Texas Homeless Education Office, THEO, until she retired in 2018. She was the first to hire me for a statewide film project, *Worn Out Welcome Mat: Texas*. I can remember how much help she provided, connecting me with incredible district homeless liaisons across that huge state. We're in constant contact. Her input on my work has been invaluable.

Slow and Steady Wins the 'Race'

The speed thing. I've always been kind of a speedster. When I was in my early tweens, my Dad took us kids to the shopping center parking lot after church. Hard to remember the old days when stores were closed on Sunday. We had a go-cart and took turns zipping around light posts and other obstacles as fast as we could. Dad (and Mom, too) were both careful, but confident and speedy drivers. So speeding is genetic for me.

Something about driving a vehicle that stretches back more than 20 feet and seems like it's wider than my given lane usually slowed me down. That's the other reason Tillie is called Tillie the Turtle. Her size and ungainliness slowed me down as with the tortoise and the hare. Turtles pick up and go, carrying their shelter on their back. With miniscule exceptions, everything I own is in my turtle. I slowed down. I became aware of my change of speed. I started noticing my surroundings. I became more comfortable with taking it slow and steady.

One of my character traits that doesn't seem to be genetic is promptness. I can remember countless times as a kid when I'd be waiting for my parents to pick me up after school, or at friend's house or at some event. I'd wait and wait. That's probably why showing up on time is important to me. It's a bit harder to do when appointments are in different states. It has required extra planning on my part. But I've succeeded. Traveling on my own, rather than flying, made arrangements easier and less stressful.

Part of my growth process in these past 15 years has been examining and reshaping my sense of self. From my Dad's gene pool, I was destined to consider myself the most important creature on the planet. I never bought that, especially on this journey. Not to say I don't value my existence, but I've taken a more muted position. I try not to overassert myself. I make a concerted effort to listen to what's in my head and heart, and to what others are saying.

Listening, hearing what others have to say, was a skill I had to work on. I've realized in my shelter days I rarely really listened. I'd hear what I wanted to hear, and often jump to judgments. Hearing is a privilege. HEAR US gave me the opportunity to hear stories. With privilege comes responsibility. Mine, as I see it, is the responsibility to share the stories I've heard over the years. This book, my videos, my blogs, my presentations are opportunities for me to share the stories so vital to understanding the plight and promise of families experiencing homelessness.

Responding to the moment gives me ultimate pleasure. Being with the family in Donna, Texas, and pretty much for all my interviews, I had no idea what I was getting into. I certainly had no idea how things would work out for the people I met. I wanted their situations to improve but I doubted my efforts would make that happen. In Donna, an impoverished community not far from Brownsville, the right people saw my video and stepped up. The family, Olga and her eight children, went from being jammed into her parent's rented ramshackle camper with a rancid-smelling plumbing leak to having a place of their own. All the kids got a chance to be successful. The mom got a good job and respect. Yay! Getting them a chance to thrive was beyond my wildest dreams.

What Scares Me?

The thing that most scared me out of my pants has always been me. I can start spinning, wanting to bail on this effort, like in Dr. Seuss's *Oh, the Places You'll Go*. In the book, he hits the idea of being scared enough that you wouldn't want to continue.

But contrary to the good Doctor's story, someone down the road between hither and yon has always come along and reinforced my sense of self, encouraging me to go on.

I can't help but think of the parents I've gotten to know and stayed in contact with over the years who have been traumatized beyond what I can grasp. They get up every day and do their best by their kids. They have less going for them in ways most can't imagine. And yet these beleaguered, courageous women and men step up for their kids. They get pummeled in every way possible: bill collectors, bureaucrats, child welfare, law enforcement, abusive exes, clueless school administrators, and more. Some may lose sight of their parental responsibilities, some don't. And if they do, it's often because they are so mentally and physically battered that they can't function. That's where our safety net needs to catch them and the kids. That's where it often fails because we—society—fail. We fail to understand that when a child or adult gets shredded by trauma, whether it is from physical, sexual and/or mental abuse, they will need help putting the pieces back together. Some will be able to. Some will not. We don't need to make it worse. We must try to make it better. We need to make sure every person has a decent place to live.

Life's a Great Balancing Act

I used to think I was an optimist by nature. That was before I entered the world of homelessness and witnessed the widespread systemic, societal dysfunction that creates and perpetuates this growing condition. Certainly, filming interviews with kids and parents experiencing homelessness has pushed me into the cynical-about-society category. It can cause a slump in my state of mind.

Fortunately, my work schedule offers more control than at a typical 9 a.m. to 5 p.m. job, whatever that means. I can adjust to a "slump" and regroup, sometimes. I try to take care of my physical health, figuring the mental health will benefit. If I get lucky, I'll be somewhere near a disc golf course where I can get exercise and let off steam. (It's a great sport, and is usually free! Check it out!) I can walk on a beach or hike in the woods.

What has proven to be therapeutic has been doing presentations along the way. I am able to share the stories I've chronicled with my vast collection of short videos. If inspired by what they've seen, I can plead with the enlightened audience to contact their congresspersons. I urge them to urge support for the Homeless Children and Youth Act which changes the definition of homelessness. I joke that I'm "Joannie Appleseed," spreading that message wherever I go.

Overall, I'm lucky to not have experienced many Seussian bang-ups and hang-ups. The bang-ups happened mostly to my rig, and those were minor. T1's fold-out step catching a curb, was a frequent annoyance that cost me $400 when I couldn't bend it back into shape. My bumps and scrapes happened when I was tired and stressed. Fortunately. Surprisingly. For all the miles I've driven, that's been it.

In August, 2019, I did humble myself with a fall that came out of nowhere in rural New York as I was on my 2020 VisionQuest. Out for an evening stroll, I stepped onto a painted handicap symbol with wet gym shoes and took a weird spill. I landed on my baby finger, seriously dislocating it. The irony of slipping on a handicap icon wasn't lost on me.

Having experienced a severe ankle dislocation many years ago, and having seen my share of bodily injuries in my shelter days, I'm not squeamish. After my tumble, I saw the bone sticking through the skin. I knew I had to do first aid. I got to my little house where I wrapped and iced it. I pulled the power cord from my camping hookup and headed to get my pinky fixed. I asked the ranger at the gate, who was chatting with a cop, where the closest medical facility was. I pointed to my injury. The cop started calling for an ambulance.

No! Thanks, I'll drive.

I got to the hospital. At the emergency room they tried to foist pain meds on me. *No.*

The doc relocated it. Wrapped it. I was on my way. Thanks to Medicare, the trip to the emergency room didn't cost me thousands. Otherwise, it could have. Something so simple and accidental could push someone into homelessness. I am painfully aware.

All Alone but Not Lonely

Alone. I wondered how I'd do with that. I had not lived alone except for short stints all my adult life. I've discovered that I like it. I enjoy people, but dealing with 100+ adults and kids for 15 years running shelters made alone time a treat. Most of the time.

I keep in contact with a small circle of family and friends. I meet new people who enrich my life. Technology has helped in that regard. My circle of friends has expanded beyond what I could have imagined. My sister laughs when I recount my routes and mention that I'll be parking in someone's driveway or at a school or shelter. "You know people everywhere!" Yup.

I plunged into Facebook back in 2007, knowing that Mark Zuckerberg's imperfect platform would keep me in contact with people across the country – people who are interested in my HEAR US efforts. I vacillate about my presence on Facebook. At first, I worried that someone could cyber-stalk me. The hacking, and potential identity theft were disconcerting at least. But I stuck with it. I've found it more useful than not in keeping contact with people across the country.

Bonuses? Facebook provided the means to connect with the first ever family I worked with way back in 1986-87 in Joliet. I've been reunited with several families from my Hesed House shelter days Those I knew as kids are now adults, with families of their own. To no surprise, the trauma they experienced as kids has impacted their adult lives. That saddens me, and motivates me to help reduce the number of kids who have to go through the awful experiences of homelessness.

I've visited with, or spoken with, women and men in crisis. I'm humbled by their universal and continuing trust in me. I know I can't fix their lives. They're doing the best they can with the hand they've been dealt. They care for their own kids, hoping to avoid homelessness again. They help others. As hard as their period of homelessness was, they learned much about survival and resilience. They've taught me a lot about the difficulties they encountered on their journeys to adulthood. It makes sense. And it's preventable.

Many Mountains in my Path

I've crossed many mountains, literally and figuratively. I think I've crossed every mountain range at least once. That alone is a challenge in my lumbering vehicles. While T1 had the power to climb, I could almost watch the fuel gauge drop towards empty. T2, with a 4-cylinder engine, requires strategy to keep going when the going gets steep. We coast downhill to get mojo to climb the next hill. Learning how to shift seven gears to slow down and save my brakes has been useful.

In 2009, I visited my long-lost cousin Kathy and her husband in California. We figured we hadn't seen each other in at least 50 years. Their driveway was so steep I couldn't possibly stay in T1. It's no fun sleeping on steep uphill, downhill or slanted surfaces. They graciously offered a bedroom. While I was there, a grandma from Texas reached out in desperation to me, crossing the "mountain" of distance to get help for her granddaughter.

Yasmin did some serious searching of the massive internet world to find me. Her voicemail message on Sunday night gave a hint of what was happening. I occasionally get voicemails from desperate parents looking for shelter. This astute grandma needed help getting her granddaughter back in school on Monday. The child had been kicked out the previous Friday. I returned Yasmin's call that night and got the details. It seemed that the school wrongly disenrolled her granddaughter. After a few minutes, I surmised that she needed a little tutorial for dealing with a recalcitrant school district. I gave her the link to our 13-minute video, REACH, which explains the basics of the McKinney-Vento Act. And I told her I'd be waiting by my phone if she needed to call while she was at the school the next morning. I suggested that she have her granddaughter with her so she could return to class. That's how sure I was that the school was wrong.

I knew I could contact my pals at THEO (Texas Homeless Education Office) if need be. But I'd wait to see how this capable grandmother would do. The next call I got from her was filled with joy and gratitude. Her granddaughter was back in school. Yay, team!

Another seemingly insurmountable mountain was in Boston. In June 2006, I was invited to speak with the editorial board of the world-esteemed Christian Science Monitor (CSM) located in the Massachusetts capital city.

I had been out East that May. I visited my friend Gail Chaddock Russell, a long-time CSM correspondent in Washington DC. Gail suggested that the CSM editorial board would benefit from my knowledge. So, she made it happen. I left DC and headed up to Boston for our June 15 meeting. That day, I allowed more than enough time to locate their downtown facility where a parking space awaited me. But the difficulty of navigating in Bean Town thwarted me, to say the least. I drove around until it made no sense to continue. I was just happy I hadn't run over any of the pedestrians in my path. Big ol' Tillie1 was not meant for Boston.

I found a parking lot of a big box store. I figured I'd leave my wheels there while I hopped a bus that I hoped would bring me somewhere near downtown. My plan was fraught with delays and stress. When I finally hopped off the bus and grabbed a cab, I got to the CSM building with five minutes to spare.

I got my sweaty-self inside. I sat at a table with about a half-dozen CSM editors and key staffers, including Marilyn Gardner, whom I had multiple contacts with over the years. I was able to downshift and get into gear for the purpose of my visit. My daunting task: I had to acquaint them with the issue of families experiencing homelessness, something it was clear they knew little about. Our session was intense, in a good way. They were extraordinarily respectful of me, probably thanks to Gail's introduction. I felt it was an extremely worthwhile visit, as exhausted as I was climbing the "mountain" that I needed to conquer to get there. The prize came when Marilyn proclaimed, "You're the nation's leading homelessness advocate!"

What happened as a result of this unprecedented meeting? Stacy Teicher Khadaroo, CSM staff writer, came out to a Boston-area campground in May 2007 and interviewed me. She did a great story, building it around a screening of my new film, *My Own Four Walls,* which she had attended. She expertly conveyed this vast, under-reported issue in a way that I've rarely seen since then.

On a personal note, she captured my state of mind when she wrote, "That's meant she hasn't had much time for campfires as she's worked 10- to 12-hour days. Whenever she started to wonder if she were crazy for voluntarily giving up her home to try to end homelessness, she'd glance up at a small photo of two young sisters she met at a shelter, and their smiles would keep her going. She's even happy to be stuck in traffic on occasion, because it gives people time to check out the huge posters promoting her cause on the back of her RV." I still have the picture of the two girls. I still need it.

Even New Jersey Was Enjoyable!

New Jersey has a bad rap. I admit I've had negative thoughts about the Garden State. When I was hired to make a statewide film on doubled up families back in 2017, I had mixed feelings, a mountain of them. But I persisted. Driving around the state, I met McKinney-Vento liaisons and connected with families to film interviews. I saw beauty in NJ in ways I couldn't have predicted. The film I made, *Worn Out Welcome Mat: Family Homelessness in New Jersey,* revealed a mountain of homelessness in that tiny state: much more than was counted by the districts there.

Uncovering that "mountain" gave me fascinating experiences, including a tremendous opportunity to share America's family homelessness story with audiences in Germany. My friend Barbara Duffield connected me with Karin Assmann, then a DC-based correspondent for Germany's Spiegel TV. Karin asked if she could follow me around for a few days and film me as well as some of the families I would be interviewing. I checked with my NJ contact and got the okay, pending the approval of the film's participants.

When we first connected, Karin and I sat and talked in T2. I had parked in the lot of the motel where she was staying. Our initial conversation gave me great hope that our time together would be good for both of us, and for my HEAR US mission. I had to overcome my tendency to let media professionals intimidate me, one of my personal mountains.

The next morning, Karin, using her Go-Pro, got footage of me driving. Then we headed to meet Max and his three kids. Once homeless, they were in their own apartment after being doubled up for years while he worked his way back from a drug-related prison stint. Their joy of having a place of their own was evident, but Max knew he was climbing a mountain that had no mercy. He depended on his masonry work schedule to make his rent: a steep $1000 a month. If he got enough hours, all that work kept him from his kids. Karin's camera work of the three kids sitting on the couch, and of other interviews we did, enhanced her Spiegel story. She also generously shared her footage with me, giving my NJ project a bonus.

Karin and I have kept in touch. I spent a few days with her in Athens, Georgia in January 2020. She is there now, teaching some very lucky journalism students at the University of Georgia.

Never Say Never!

Before March 2020, if you suggested I go anywhere near Dallas for any purpose, I'd say NEVER! I'd been caught in Dallas traffic enough. I've been turned off by the area's aura of opulence. I'd put Dallas on my list of "never." But when Dallas City Council Member Cara Mendelsohn contacted me about making a 2020 stop in Big D, I said yes. Cara and I went back a long time, to my first round of travel when she ran a shelter on the outskirts of that city.

Cara arranged a film screening and a forum for representatives of local programs to share their info. Perfect! She lined up a delightful family for me to stay with. I parked in their driveway despite invitations for me to stay in their guest room. Cara and I had time to talk. We brainstormed ways to get Dallas to be more helpful for homeless families, youth and adults. She leads the charge on this issue for the City Council and has accomplished some jaw-dropping milestones due to her inability to take "no" for an answer.

Then covid-19 exploded. Among other things, it destroyed my plans to meet with city staff for a training session on homelessness. She later arranged a virtual presentation on family homelessness with her constituents in July 2020. That helped them understand the importance of opening a family shelter in their district. It's hard to imagine that Dallas, a city of more than 1.3 million and a poverty rate of over 21%, has only one family shelter. Pre-Covid, that was a horrible reality. I'm hoping Cara's model, using a former motel, will start an epidemic of shelters and services for the thousands of Dallas families who will find themselves unhoused.

The Biggest Mountain of All

As I sat in T2 working on this book in my friend's driveway in Kansas, I could not help but be dismazed about the future of America, and the world, as we climb this mountain of an unprecedented disaster: Covid19. Every day I read news stories that shake me to my core. Sure, I'm concerned about my own health, and the health and well-being of my loved ones. But I can't help but envision a seismic growth in homelessness and poverty as this unfathomable crisis continues. The flattening of the curve, which to me seems like a mountain, will be a long road. The consequential human tragedies and accompanying economic destruction guarantee an increase of homelessness beyond imagining.

Evictions, some legal, many not, are pushing people to the streets. States and municipalities have placed too-short moratoriums on them. Shelters, filled to beyond capacity, have been trying to figure out how to safely distance their patrons, volunteers, and staff while record numbers of people turn to them for help.

Motels, housing those who HUD doesn't consider homeless as well as those placed by agencies with HUD dollars, are temporarily holding back the flow of homeless families.

When the imminent danger is declared over, many families will be thrust back into homelessness. Newly homeless families, those who lost their housing in economic carnage, will join them. In the first months of Covid, many shelters did not accept new families, understandable considering the risks and the need to social distance. What do the newly-homeless families do when they can't get the meager help that once existed? Resources for emergency shelter have been depleted during the first months of the pandemic as shelters rethought their models and turned to motels to protect their families. Congress, in what seems to be a perennially clueless mindset, is reluctant to provide more help.

Invisible Enigma

Our nation has denied the scope of family homelessness for decades. Ever since the 80s, families have done their best to survive. Some have ended up in unimaginably horrible conditions. Thousands of discarded people, including families, tumbled onto Skid Row in LA, or into campgrounds. Such locals reflect the jettisoned nature of these denizens of poverty. Others live in vermin-infested abandoned buildings to escape ever worsening conditions. Still more persevere stealthily, hiding their families' homelessness from authorities in an ironic effort to protect them. Countless others bounce around from couch, to motels, to vehicles, to shelters and around again, wearing out their welcome, climbing out of homelessness only to fall back into it.

Evictions. Economic demise. Family breakups. Job loss. Illness. Stress. Trauma. Abject poverty. Criminal records. Addiction. Abuse. Hopelessness.

Those realities, alone and in combination, will explode in the next weeks and months as a side effect of our pandemic-wrecked nation. I'd like to think we'll rise to the occasion and fend off the worst of this inevitable disaster, but nothing I've seen so far gives me hope.

Another issue, a daunting one when I give it thought, is how many of these upended households will lose their right to vote? Knowing how stressful and disruptive pre-homelessness is, the last thing many families think of is safeguarding their important documents, like IDs and voter cards. Mail gets lost in the shuffle. Ballot mailing regulations are complicated. This is the kind of glitch that will likely disenfranchise a wide swath of voters.

Congress continues to figure ways to enrich the wealthy. They siphon billions and billions away from those who need it most: those trying to survive wave after wave of disasters. The government's blatant efforts to channel money to the very rich seems as unstoppable as billionaires' shamelessly grab stimulus dollars to increase their billions.

We've seen the same thing happen before. During the Great Recession of '08, our "leaders" upended the housing market, shredded consumer protections, and poured money into the banks that caused this economic meltdown. At the same time, they rewarded Wall Street and giant corporations for their nefarious contribution to that disastrous period. Those atrocities were nothing compared to what we're seeing in 2020.

I don't want to continue my rant about this inevitable direction. I'd also love to be wrong. I can hope that enlightened leadership on all levels will read the text book I co-authored,

Changing the Paradigm of Homelessness. If they do, we might not go down the same path that has proven to be cataclysmic for families and individuals experiencing homelessness.

The horrible events surrounding the murder of George Floyd by Minneapolis cops on May 25, 2020, has capsized our flailing democracy. Once again, racism—as exemplified by police power over Black people—spills blood across our land. Protestors rage, mostly peaceful. The threat posed by violent interlopers disrupts and destroys their nonviolent efforts. Looters—those breaking store windows and scooping up merchandise—cause outrage. Meanwhile the mega-looters, those in power making off with billions of pandemic relief dollars, escape unscathed.

My cynical thinking—ala Charlie Brown being taunted to kick the football by Lucy—is *here we go again.* Another era of racial unrest that won't get to the root causes of our anger.

To be continued…

What Mountain Will I Climb?

I'm not sure. I've got a desire to film family homelessness as caused and impacted by the coronavirus. In addition to the housing hardships, reports that children's health is severely affected by covid-19 make this even more of a crisis. But I don't want to endanger my health in the process. I've got time to ponder how to use my talents and passion to make a mark on this issue. As it has every time I've hit this point in decision making, I expect a sign will appear.

An anonymous quote, "We are where we should be, doing what we should be doing, otherwise we'd be somewhere else doing something else," adorns one of the pictures in my little house. I've wrestled with that sentiment more times than I could count. I'm here now. Where will I be next? I unashamedly say, "I haven't a clue."

Perhaps home is not a place but simply an irrevocable condition.

– James Baldwin

CHAPTER 12
Future Roadmap

In 15 years of nomadic existence, I've never stayed three months in one spot. The combination of coronavirus followed by widespread and unpredictable racial unrest acted as "The Boot," locking me in place in my friend's driveway. My book would not have happened without this speedbump.

Way back in the early 1990s, when I first began advocating for the educational rights of students experiencing homelessness, I never would have envisioned how far my involvement would take me. I'd like to say the fight is over. That we won. Now I can move to other challenges. But that's not the case. What we've done is open a can of worms.

It's vital that we bump up HUD's pathetically inadequate standards to include the millions of families and youth they've chosen to ignore. That would spark the systemic change. It would begin to address the much-overlooked problem of family and youth homelessness. Oh hell, let's open it up all the way. Let's put on the table the overarching injustice of poverty.

The brutal murder of George Floyd is the current event seismic enough to stimulate focus on a sore subject: abject poverty. His death, with the seemingly infinite litany of victims of violence afflicting people of color, lit that fire. Our disaster-of-a-president ineptly claimed that the late Mr. Floyd is smiling at our economy. I'd say maybe George Floyd and all whose lives have been cruelly erased deserve credit for shifting how we see poverty and racism. It's kind of like finding "good" in the coronavirus. It has pulled back the curtain on family homelessness.

This weighty topic of poverty certainly requires a force far greater than me. What I bring to the table is my 15 years gathering stories about family and youth poverty and homelessness. My disparate cast of cogent spokespersons from across the country must be heard and heeded. Anecdotal, the social scientists would shout.

Yes, but....

I've always marveled at insights from those who don't get to sit at the table of policymaking. I've been constantly dismazed by the widespread exclusion of these true connoisseurs of paucity. It takes a certain level of personal and professional security to hear what needs to be said. We must heed criticisms from those inside the system. My independent position, my commitment, as our HEAR US mission statement professes, is to give voice and visibility to children and youth experiencing homelessness. This directive has provided me the opportunity to invite the experts to the table. My travels offered me the opportunity to hear, chronicle, and share what those "in the system" want the policymakers and the public to know.

Astute Assessment by a Driven Grandma

One of my favorite poverty-philosophers is Melissa N (Chapter 4, 7). A Mama Bear, her poignant Facebook posts describe the challenges of being a single, resource-challenged grandparent with kids and grandkids in her care. You don't come between her and her "cubs." I've known her longer than any other HEAR US parent. Hers was my first family to interview. I've kept up with her since.

The difficult task of quickly setting up e-learning systems caught school systems by surprise with this pandemic outbreak. Few realized the depth and breadth of the internet divide before schools were closed across the land. I've interviewed plenty of parents and kids who talk about their inability to cyber-connect. That was before schools shut down. The general insensitivity, or at least cluelessness, to the logistics and expense of this is widespread. When schools announced, via email and texts, their plan for e-learning, they were not prepared for the extensive outrage and frustration.

Melissa posted her thoughts on Facebook. I, too, shared her post on my FB pages. With her permission I share it again, here.

So now children will be marked absent from school on a weekly basis if their parent/caregiver is unable to make contact with the child's teacher. This virus and all it has caused, changed and/or taken from people is NOT the children's or the families fault. Sure...dish out more stress, anxiety and expectations that put the struggling at even greater risk of falling to the effects of yet another unexpected and torrential storm. Remember: Some people were barely budgeted to appease 'Peter and Paul.' Phones and internet are being turned off and many homes don't have computers, people are forced to live doubled and tripled up because of health, financial or safety reasons.

This is NOT the time to add insult to injury or assume every household has the means to maintain contact with anyone. *Instructional packets are appreciated. Much gratitude and respect go out to the Teachers, Support staff and administrators who are stepping up to provide educational,* *nutritional and moral support to all the children they serve with heart and passion daily but the WHOLE picture is so very different now for everyone. You don't count absences when Hurricanes take out our lines of communication.*

Just STOP, think outside the boxes of Standard Operating Procedures and realize that not EVERY family has the resources or support to do much more than try to survive this. *When the children come back, they will be expected to change gears again. This should be addressed and cared for long-term as the truly unexpected and traumatic event it is! Most were NOT prepared for a Pandemic...on any level!*

Melissa's family's reality includes very limited monthly income for her son's disability. Her broken-down car recently died. Her 15-year old FEMA trailer barely shelters them from the elements. When I visited her remote home recently, I couldn't get internet on my phone. She has to pay about $100 a month to stay connected. That's a big chunk of her family's monthly income. Melissa successfully pursued her college degree back in 2006. One of the most astute parents I've met, she has been dealt a hand that would make me crumble. I often think she'd be a tremendous legislator. But she's an impoverished single-mom and grandma, who must care for a teen son with neurological challenges. She patches together a safety net around her two daughters. Both in their 20s, they and their babies depend on her. Melissa does all of this in the middle of nowhere—25+ miles from her little town of Milton, FL.

After their previous trailer park was condemned, Melissa had to find another place to park this ramshackle home-sweet-home. She lucked out when she found a little enclave owned by a friend. She stood in front of the Santa Rosa County board and made a strong, desperate plea for $5,000 to move her trailer. Plenty was riding on this last ditch effort. If she failed, her entire extended family would have been homeless. Again. She succeeded! surprising even me. I was even more surprised when her dilapidated trailer survived the move.

Delightfully, where Melissa and her kids landed has a lot to offer. There's plenty of room for the kids to romp. With caring adults around, it's a relatively safe and controlled area. There's a river to fish. They can skip rocks. The one trouble is, the distance from schools and stores demands a reliable vehicle and gas money—two things lacking from this intrepid mother's arsenal.

I worry that maybe her luck is running out. In March 2020, the property owner balked at how many people were living in Melissa's trailer. Sure, that's a reason for concern. But we're the midst of a pandemic. We've been urged to stay home. Not long into the outbreak, Melissa's daughter, child, and a young friend, all of whom had nowhere to go to quarantine themselves, showed up at Melissa's doorstep. What was she to do? The property owner wants to charge her an extra $100 per person per month for lot rent. Insane!

Melissa, in true Mama Bear fashion, has hunkered down to take care of the most essential. She's keeping her family from being homeless again. She juggles the immediate needs of her kids and grandkids. With distance learning replacing classrooms, devices and internet connections are vital. Her old laptop worked for the younger kids, but she needed a computer for her 17-year-old son with autism. I was happy to provide the connection to make that happen. She began homeschooling four kids at four different grade levels.

They have a jump on social distancing, which I counted as a plus until she let me know her Covid test came back positive in mid-July 2020. Although she's had plenty of practice surviving, the brutal nature of this virus changes the odds. So far, inexplicably, she's the only one in their tiny trailer household knocked flat by Covid. She messaged me:

You know the leeches don't stop sucking and the collectors don't pause to give you a break but I'll take it given the alternative. To have to tell my son I can't hug him, watch a video or animation he created or even be close to him; to have to maintain a distance from my granddaughter, to say no to sharing the couch to watch a movie, no to fixing her hair, playing a game or making slime with her and then she can't even go outside to play with her friends...well, it's the mental and emotional torment that comes with this battle and then there is little to no energy within you and you are still required to be the caregiver.

The fact that she and her family have to cope with what yet another mammoth challenge seems profoundly unfair. That she has the mental wherewithal awes me.

They're Intrepid, I'm a Wuss

That's the thing about the families I've met: they're intrepid. "Resolutely fearless. Dauntless," in a way that inspires me. I can't count the times along this 15-year odyssey that I've felt lost and pathetic. *What the hell am I doing with my life? Why am I sleeping in some godforsaken parking lot in the middle of nowhere on my way to capture a story from someone who few care about?*

Where the hell am I? Here I am waking up in yet another place where I have no internet.

Then I'd get to my destination-du jour, meet my interviewee, set up my video camera, and get blown away by the story they share. That's when I'd know why I was where I was, doing what I was doing. I've vacillated between a sense of awe and a sense of *aw shit* on any given day. Multiple times a day.

Mile by Mile

The one phenomenon that continues to fascinate me about long distance travel is my concept of "here to there." Depending on my state of mind, I can get lost, Zen-like, in the process of covering the miles. It's thinking time. I often scribble notes (less annoying than dictating to Siri) that capture my best thoughts.

Or I can let the miles grind interminably. I can't tell you how many hours I've inched my way from my starting point to my end point feeling like each mile was gnawing at my soul. I know I can't get to there without being here, moving forward, one mile at a time. So, too, our progress on systemic social issues. Making a significant dent in family homelessness requires relentless patience and planning.

Sooner, rather than later, we need to get HUD to redefine homelessness to match the US Department of Education definition. They must include the millions of families and youth who lack a place to live but are not staying in shelters or on the streets.

TAKE ACTION! To get that to happen, go to www.helphomelesskids.org and click on Take Action. In less than 30 seconds you can urge your congressional representatives to support our legislation: the Homeless Children and Youth Act.

We could use my mile-by-mile approach for family homelessness and poverty issues:

- Where are we going? Lay out our route, our goals.
- What "supplies" are needed? Identify needs and potential resources.
- Who is best to "drive" the different segments? As with driving, some are better able to handle certain challenges.
- How do we adjust to uniqueness of rural, suburban, and urban "traffic?" The challenges are not one-size-fits-all.
- What's needed to get started? Fill up the tank. Tune up the engine. Don't procrastinate!
  - Get moving! Allow the poverty-experts to drive, and navigate. Provide the roadside assistance for the inevitable breakdown. Make sure the drivers get adequate rest and refreshment.
  - OK, I won't belabor the metaphor, but it does apply.

Unexpected Obstacles

The incalculable agonies of 2020 tumble like boulders off a mountainside onto our nation's highway. Covid-19 upended millions of lives in the U.S. and billions beyond. Our borders, with the untended oozing scars of xenophobia's injustice, continue to fester. Racial turmoil, ignited by, among other things, failure of law and order to balance the scales of justice, brought us to our knees. These, and countless other, unexpected "detours" have disrupted our already bumpy route.

I'm not sure what these significant events will mean for my HEAR US mission. I know my excursion, and my mission, won't be easy. To propel me forward, I only have to reflect back at a treasure chest of experiences. I've experienced a life-changing adventure. One I could never have imagined. Now, I must look forward.

Personally, I find myself more determined than ever to focus my energies and talents on the unfinished business of getting our nation on track to address family homelessness. I'm not ready to retire. What will the next phase of my travels—my life and my time behind the wheel—look like? I have no clue.

Rearview Mirror Reflections

Pre-coronavirus, I prided myself on self-sufficiency and preparation. I hunkered in groceries and essential supplies: stuff I knew I'd need and maybe might not be able to get in the middle of nowhere. I took care of mechanical responsibilities—vehicle and equipment—to make sure they'd work when I needed them.

One of my quirks? When I was afraid of running out of an essential supply, food, water, propane, etc., I experienced what I describe as over-anxiety. Fortunately, I'd usually pick up on my edginess and identify the source. That helps a bit. I never suffered from deprivation. How do families cope with not having a home? Or not being able to feed their kids? Or any of the endless anxiety-producing realities they encounter daily?

When I feel like a useless schmuck, which doesn't happen often, but creeps in on occasion, my "coping mechanism tool box" contains a few useful strategies. Music. My go-to selections of late tend to be Carrie Newcomer, especially her latest release, *The Point of Arrival*. Sara Thomsen's music has long worked wonders. Her most recent, *Song Like a Seed*, can clear my head and heart. My Spotify feed contains an eclectic collection that nourishes my spirit. Yes, I sing aloud. Good that I mostly travel alone!

I learned long ago—pre-HEAR US—that watching regular programing on TV did nothing for me, especially with the onslaught of Big Pharma and political campaign ads. Not having a TV has saved me sanity and money. I can stream movies on my iPad or computer. My assorted reading materials, which typically I pick up before bed, reflect my desire to ingest meaningful and calming thoughts.

Whenever my spirits are flagging, I invariably hear from someone who cares about what I do. They tell me so in no uncertain terms. Their words fill my psychological tank again. I've gotten much better at noticing when something is off—in my rig and in my head. Not that I have it perfectly down pat, but I've improved at heeding the warning signs and doing something about them.

On-Time Delivery

One of my big concerns when starting this venture, and continuing to this day, has always been maintaining my integrity. I want to do right by the families I interview. I want to represent them honestly, not distorting their circumstances for any reason. I also want them to be completely comfortable about the filming process from beginning to end. A handful of times my subject backed out. They didn't need to share their reasons. I hope I eased their anxiety about their decision.

When contracting with a state or other organization for a project, my standard is: I do what I agree to, how they want, on time. So far, so good on that commitment. My biased personal assessment of my video projects? I'm proud of them. They honestly reflect my subjects and give an accurate insight of their experience of homelessness. Feelings about what school means comes through loud and clear. The most important feedback I've received has been from the stars of my films, and that feedback has been extraordinarily positive. These tangibles are important in my wabi-sabi world.

Rear-Ended

I don't deal well with political deception and devious motivations. I don't like drama. I believe most problems can be solved with a combination of effort, resources, and political or personal goodwill. The covid-19 outbreak, appallingly mishandled from the beginning in the U.S., validated my negative assessment of our so-called leaders. Their fear-baiting, inconsistency, and confusing lack of direction has contributed mightily to mental duress. Mine included.

I worry not for myself but for those I know and love. I have utter disdain for the predominant governing forces in this covid-19 era. Things weren't going too well, to say the least, before this crisis. Now sanity is pushed to the edge. Before 2020, the prospect of destruction of the world order—on every front—hung like a ferocious storm cloud. Then we learned about the devastation an invisible virus might wreak on all of us. With every news source streaming health-related horror stories at us, I felt doom and gloom overcoming my psyche. At least I recognized that I was heading down that dark path and jerked myself back.

I agonize over the plight of families and youth I've met, and those I know are out there across the land. They navigate their rugged day-to-day road. Some make tremendous strides, overcoming their hardships and advancing toward their dreams. Now they've been rear-ended by a renegade semi-tractor trailer driven by Queen Coronavirus.

Make no mistake. Our nation's racial furor—stemming from centuries of neglected systemic flaws—has a major impact on poverty and homelessness. I'll let others more qualified than me expound on this topic. But I will unequivocally state that the underlying causes of racial injustice, and their impact on people of color today, contribute profoundly to the suffering of families experiencing homelessness. We each contribute to the detriment or betterment of racial justice. We all must find our shortcomings and address them!

My Travel Toolkit

Some travelers go to extensive levels to prepare for a long trip, ready in case the worst might happen. I made sure I have an assortment of flashlights and basic tools. Oh yeah, and duct tape. To bolster my sense of direction especially on cloudy days, I'm happy to have a vehicle with a working compass (one of my favorite T2 features!), my iPhone's GPS app, and an atlas.

What might be more notable are the few things I *didn't* bring on this journey.

- **A sense of importance.** No one asked me to do this project. It was my concoction, born out of a 2-sided dilemma: 1) to make a meaningful contribution when it comes to the issue of homeless kids; and 2) to work without the fear losing my job, or at least where it would be up to me to make or break my career. My takeaway: I've learned how extensive family homelessness is. I've learned how extended my family and friends circle is. And how essential they are to me.
- **A sense of knowing what I'm doing.** Nah, I never knew. My life is filled with escapades that I was clueless about at the beginning. I was utterly clueless about the big RV things: knowing how to handle the RV aspects, driving, parking, weather challenges, rules and social acceptance, maintenance, etc. Ditto for the filmmaking tasks: how to film, equipment functions, techniques, interviewing skills, editing and

composition. The important but peripheral things—administrative tasks, doing presentations, website maintenance, writing blogs and articles—were manageable. Any or all of these tasks would cause me anxiety on any given day. But I always had help, those I knew were there or someone who popped out of nowhere. And now I kind of know what I need to know.

- **A sense of knowing where I was going.** Sure, I had destinations, and I found them. I did what I needed to do when I got there. But most of the time I just had to trust that I'd know where I needed to go. That was a fascinating feeling when I was sitting in a part of the country where I knew no one, and I was far from anything that resembles life as I knew it. When people ask me what's next, I have to say, "I don't know."
Do I have a 5-year plan? 1-year plan? Nope. That's what makes most grant applications so difficult. Funders like to know I've got a plan. My plan is flexibility to respond when and where I am needed.

- **A sense of knowing I'd have the financial support to continue.** Support was a biggie, for obvious reasons. Really, from the time I first pulled out of Naperville in November 2005, driving a humongous house-on-wheels, I felt I was in the middle of nowhere. I was unknown to more than a handful of people. Those who have generously donated to this cause have bolstered my faith in humanity more than you'd ever know! I know I have what I need for today. That one-day-at-a-time approach is the best I can do.

- **A sense of thinking many people cared about what I was doing.** Again, since this was my driven dream, not the result of an edict from above, I lacked the sense of confidence that a lot of people were cheering me on. I knew those I interviewed cared. That was usually enough for me. Usually. I continue to be humbled when I hear what my efforts have meant. I remind myself that I didn't do this to garner praise.

What has bolstered me on my travels?

- **A sense of awe.** I can get choked up about what I see and who I meet. I've seen beauty in places I'd never expect. A field of multi-colored irises waving in the afternoon sun on a dirt road detour. A creek keeping me company on a backroad. The endless expanse of hills and mountains, the infinite ribbon of highway—vastness that reminds me of my smallness.
- I've met people whose devotion to life and family far exceeds what I have ever felt, and many have become treasured friends. I've witnessed the conversion factor. That's when someone previously opposed to doing right by a kid or family somehow sees the light and becomes an ardent advocate. I've stood proudly by as a parent or youth spoke up about their situation in front of audiences that would intimidate the average person.
- **A sense of gratitude**. Oh my, this is a biggie. I've become almost hyper-aware of what I have, so much compared to what little so many have. My many occasions of relatively minimal discomfort get diminished by my awareness of how others suffer—cold, heat, hunger, somewhere to be welcome, a safe and comfortable place to sleep. I've felt the love and support of so many that I should be flogged for having any doubt about my efforts.
- **A strong sense of support from my board and close friends.** Those who understand why I do what I'm doing know how important it is to the families and youth who benefit by greater understanding of their needs. From them I get an incalculable amount of support. Financial. Time. Expertise. And the indescribable web of friendship that's there when I know it or not.

It's just a start. The fuel for the engine.

ENDORSEMENTS

Dismazed and Driven joins America's literature of life on the road. It captures America's spirit of the search for meaning while one explores. It departs from the selfish part of road literature because it's about one person's dedication to people caught in poverty and inequality. Diane Nilan travels to meet and record the experiences of families and their children who are homeless, with tenderness and sadness, but tinged with hope. A lovely read.

Joe Willard,**Vice President, People's Emergency Center, Philadelphia, Pennsylvania**

Dismazed and Driven will pull you into the world of the author and the homeless families she seeks out. Join Diane Nilan as she continues to drive dismazed, sharing her life and stories and anecdotes of families that reveal disastrous and overlooked conditions. This book paints a realistic, sometimes startling, and often touching picture of homelessness in America that is not common knowledge. But once you know, you will never forget.

Judy Borich, **Middle River Press, Oakland Park, Florida**

Diane Nilan's memoir, *Dismazed and Driven*, is a powerful blend of storytelling and call for social justice for our most vulnerable and disenfranchised. A must-read for those seeking insight into the deleterious effects of homelessness on families, children and youth here in the United States.

Dr. Anita C. Levine, **Professor of Elementary Education, SUNY Oneonta, New York**

There is no one who has devoted more time and energy to bringing attention to the crisis of homeless children and families in America. From the "happiest place on Earth" to the Pacific Northwest, Diane has travelled the highways and backroads giving voice to the voiceless. This recounting of her adventures is heartwarming, poignant, and powerful.

Heather Denny, **Montana State Coordinator for Homeless**

BIBLIOGRAPHY

Chicago Tribune. (2020, August 5). *Homeless Kids Test School Boundaries.* Retrieved from Chicago Tribune : https://www.chicagotribune.com/news/ct-xpm-1993-09-04-9309040075-story.html

CNN. (2020, April 9). *Millions of low-income children are still waiting for federal food aid.* Retrieved from CNN Politics: https://www.cnn.com/2020/04/09/politics/school-children-federal-food-aid-covid-crisis/index.html

Collins, M. (2020, April 15). *Even Without a Home, We Always Had a Family Meal.* Retrieved from The New York Times: https://www.nytimes.com/2020/04/15/parenting/misha-collins-supernatural-family-meal.html?fbclid=IwAR3KWwVRIZnwhoVc_A_EJypwyib4VX7pQK50Z tXlS-EqRpbaOROah8HzTUQ

Diane Nilan. (2020, August 5). *2020 VisionQuest.* Retrieved from HEAR US Inc.: https://www.hearus.us/projects/awareness/2020.html

First Focus. (2020, April 14). *Congressional Testimony. Comment: Considerations for Additional Measures of Poverty.* Retrieved from First Focus on Children: https://firstfocus.org/resources/congressional-testimony/comment-considerations-for-additional-measures-of-poverty

HEAR US Inc. . (2013, January 5). *Doggone Shame--Vet and Sons Homeless in Mobile, AL.* Retrieved from YouTube: https://youtu.be/UTSRb5rKuSE

HEAR US Inc. (2013, April 13). *We had it one day--Lupe's story.* Retrieved from YouTube: https://youtu.be/IW2ATWBbbmA

HEAR US Inc. (2013, October 22). *Worn Out Welcome Mat - Leia and Family.* Retrieved from YouTube: https://youtu.be/Z33aZS1i6Bo

HEAR US Inc. (2015, November 30). *Worn Out Welcome Mat - Kansas .* Retrieved from YouTube: https://youtu.be/0dl_N-wrHWI

HEAR US Inc. (2015, May 14). *Worn Out Welcome Mat - KS: Marine Mama.* Retrieved from YouTube: https://www.youtube.com/watch?v=x7J87hj01gw

HEAR US Inc. (2015, May 14). *Worn Out Welcome Mat -KS: Melissa--It's All About Sex.* Retrieved from YouTube: https://youtu.be/jvgLH6H-cho

HEAR US Inc. (2016, July 5). *Christina 'Our Worst Fear'.* Retrieved from YouTube: https://www.youtube.com/watch?v=44rt-9-icH4

HEAR US Inc. (2018, March 25). *Worn Out Welcome Mat: Family Homelessness in New Jersey.* Retrieved from Vimeo: https://vimeo.com/261706278

HEAR US Inc. (2019, December 23). *Parking Lot Survival: Homeless Family with Nowhere to Go.* Retrieved from YouTube: https://youtu.be/rJun5ZtcPgY

HEAR US Inc. (2020, August 6). *Babes of Wrath.* Retrieved from HEAR US.us: https://www.hearus.us/projects/babestour.html

HEAR US Inc. (2020, January 11). *Desperate in OR: Homeless Families and Youth.* Retrieved from YouTube: https://www.youtube.com/watch?v=sURJhYK0pWc

HEAR US Inc. (2020, August 5). *How Many Homeless Kids?* Retrieved from HEAR US Inc.: https://www.hearus.us/understand-homelessnses/howmany.html

HEAR US Inc. (2020, January 6). *Invisible Homeless Families.* Retrieved from YouTube: https://youtu.be/BcM25df7eXM

HEAR US Inc. (2020, August 5). *My Biggest Fear.* Retrieved from Vimeo: https://vimeo.com/261206319

HEAR US Inc. (2020, August 5). *My Own Four Walls.* Retrieved from HEAR US Inc.: https://www.hearus.us/projects/awareness/my-own-four-walls-video.html

HEAR US Inc. (2020, August 6). *on the edge.* Retrieved from HEAR US: https://www.hearus.us/projects/awareness/ote.html

HEAR US Inc. (2020, August 6). *Other Stuff.* Retrieved from www.hearus.us: https://www.hearus.us/understand-homelessnses/causes.html

HEAR US Inc. (2020, August 5). *Positively Homeless: Family Homelessness in America.* Retrieved from Vimeo: https://vimeo.com/351811507

HEAR US Inc. (2020, February 19). *Ride It Out--Hurricane Michael's Carnage.* Retrieved from YouTube: https://youtu.be/urzJR08pmVc

HUD. (2020, August 5). *Homelessness Prevention and Rapid Re-Housing Program.* Retrieved from HUD Exchange: https://www.hudexchange.info/programs/hprp/

HUD. (2020, January 7). *HUD Releases 2019 Annual Homeless Assessment Report.* Retrieved from HUD.gov: https://www.hud.gov/press/press_releases_media_advisories/HUD_No_20_003

HUD. (2020, August 6). *Mission.* Retrieved from HUD.GOV: https://www.hud.gov/about/mission

Illinois General Assembly. (2020, August 5). *Illinois Compiled Statutes.* Retrieved from Illinois General Assembly: https://www.ilga.gov/legislation/ilcs/ilcs5.asp?ActID=1013&ChapterID=17.125

Khadaroo, S. T. (2007, May 24). *Homeless children tell their stories.* Retrieved from The Christian Science Monitor: https://www.csmonitor.com/2007/0524/p14s01-legn.html

National Alliance to End Homelessness. (2012, January 18). *Changes in the HUD Definition of "Homeless".* Retrieved from National Alliance to End Homelessness: https://endhomelessness.org/resource/changes-in-the-hud-definition-of-homeless/

National Center on Homeless Education. (2020, August 5). *National Overview.* Retrieved from National Center for Homeless Education: http://profiles.nche.seiservices.com/ConsolidatedStateProfile.aspx

NCHE. (2020, August 5). *National Overview.* Retrieved from National Center for Homeless Education at SERVE: http://profiles.nche.seiservices.com/ConsolidatedStateProfile.aspx

Nilan, D. (2009, April 30). *The Longest 100 Days--Now What?* Retrieved from invisible homeless kids: https://invisible-homeless-kids.blogspot.com/2009/04/longest-100-days-now-what.html

Nilan, D. (2010, November 22). *Land of 'Yes Ma'am' and Tragedies.* Retrieved from invisible homeless kids: https://invisible-homeless-kids.blogspot.com/2010/

Nilan, D. (2010, January 11). *Poverty and Homelessness: Call It What It Is!* Retrieved from invisible homeless kids: https://invisible-homeless-kids.blogspot.com/2010/01/poverty-and-homelessness-call-it-what.html

Nilan, D. (2018, March 17). *Medium Diane Nilan.* Retrieved from Medium: https://medium.com/@dianehearus/whats-criminal-the-way-we-treat-homeless-families-601c610ef926

Nilan, D. (2019, September 19). *Hungry Kids Make Poor Learners.* Retrieved from Medium.com: https://medium.com/@dianehearus/hungry-kids-make-poor-learners-36a999c6274c

Nilan, D. (2020, August 6). *Diane Nilan.* Retrieved from Facebook: https://www.facebook.com/diane.nilan

Nilan, D. (2020, February 13). *Mercedes Benz Sprinter Warning Light (& more) Hell.* Retrieved from Medium.com: https://medium.com/@dianehearus/mercedes-benz-sprinter-warning-light-more-hell-625853729798

Pat LaMarche. (2010, February 18). *Palin's palm problem.* Retrieved from Bangor Daily News: https://bangordailynews.com/2010/02/18/opinion/palins-palm-problem/

Poor People's Campaign. (2020, August 5). *Our Demands.* Retrieved from Poor People's Campaign: https://www.poorpeoplescampaign.org/about/our-demands/

Randall, K. (2010, January 7). *Homelessness, utility shutoffs lead to house fires, freezing deaths. US cold snap highlights depth of social crisis.* Retrieved from Axis of Logic: http://axisoflogic.com/artman/publish/Article_58033.shtml

Research Center National Overview. (2020, August 5). Retrieved from Meet Alice: https://www.unitedforalice.org/national-overview

SchoolHouse Connection. (2020, August 5). *McKinney-Vento Act: Two-page Summary.* Retrieved from SchoolHouse Connection:

https://www.schoolhouseconnection.org/mckinney-vento-act-two-page-summary/

SchoolHouse Connection. (2020, August 5). *Take Action to Help Homeless Children and Youth.* Retrieved from SchoolHouse Connection: https://www.schoolhouseconnection.org/policy-advocacy/hcya/

Spiegel. (2017, December 12). *Obdachlose Kinder.* Retrieved from Spiegel Panorama: https://www.spiegel.de/video/von-der-gesellschaft-vergessen-obdachlose-kinder-video-1821064.html

Thomsen, S. (2004). *Holy Angels.* Retrieved from sarathomsen: https://sarathomsen.com/track/1916933/holy-angels

U.S. Congress. (2019, April 1). *H.R.2001 - Homeless Children and Youth Act of 2019.* Retrieved from Congress.gov: https://www.congress.gov/bill/116th-congress/house-bill/2001/text

U.S. Department of Agriculture. (2020, August 5). *Supplemental Nutrition Assistance Program (SNAP).* Retrieved from USDA Food and Nutrition Services: https://www.fns.usda.gov/snap/supplemental-nutrition-assistance-program

U.S. Government Printing Office. (2007, October 16). *Reauthorization of the McKinney-Vento Homeless Assistance Act, Part II.* Retrieved from www.govinfo.gov: https://www.govinfo.gov/content/pkg/CHRG-110hhrg39908/html/CHRG-110hhrg39908.htm

University of Wisconsin-Madison. (2020, August 5). *How Is Poverty Measured?* Retrieved from Institute For Research on Poverty: https://www.irp.wisc.edu/resources/how-is-poverty-measured/

Wikipedia. (2020, August 5). *Self Storage.* Retrieved from Wikipedia: https://en.wikipedia.org/wiki/Self_storage

---

APPENDIX

Companion Books and Resources

HEAR US resources:

If you find yourself interested in the topic of family homelessness when you're done with my account, check out our textbook, *Changing the Paradigm of Homelessness* (Routledge, 2019), by Professors Yvonne Vissing, Christopher Hudson and yours truly.

My first book, *Crossing the Line: Taking Steps to End Homelessness* (Booklocker, 2005), a timeless, reader-friendly account of people I met in my years running a shelter, will give you invaluable context to some of the topics I get into in *Dismazed and Driven*.

Check out my HEAR US website, www.hearus.us, where you can access videos I've made and other resources about family and youth homelessness. My Facebook page is another good spot if you're so inclined (Nilan, Diane Nilan, 2020).

Post-Covid World

Here's a list of what I'd like to see as immediate improvements to the world that surrounds homeless families and youth. If you're looking for more on the topic, remember our textbook, *Changing the Paradigm of Homelessness*, which I co-wrote with my esteemed colleagues, Professors Yvonne Vissing and Christopher Hudson.

MY BASIC INGREDIENTS OF A POST-COVID019-LESS-HOMELESS WORLD:

- Change the way we <u>define homelessness, the campaign</u> I've been involved with for years, so we don't exclude millions who have no homes.
- Offer multiple housing solutions — not one-size-fits-all — for people of all income-challenged levels.
- Accommodate those in the work world who want to escape homelessness.
- Make arrangements in the best interest of <u>kids</u> of all ages.
- Accept that people will stumble and fall, don't penalize them, and give them the opportunity(ies) to rise with dignity.
- Make sure every person has access to bathrooms, hygiene, a safe place to rest, health care, nutritional food, mental health services, etc.
- Protect access to education for students of all ages. Consider their needs for tech access, year-round living arrangements, transportation, and childcare, to name a few.
- Build a strong safety net so those on the edge don't fall into homelessness. (Eviction prevention, debt forgiveness, utility assistance, legal help, etc.)
- Establish basic livable levels of income, access to health care, transportation options, quality child care, healthy and affordable nutrition.
- Provide for the elderly and infirm in a humane manner.

HUD MISSION

(HUD, 2020)

Home / About HUD / Mission

MISSION

HUD's mission is to create strong, sustainable, inclusive communities and quality affordable homes for all. HUD is working to strengthen the housing market to bolster the economy and protect consumers; meet the need for quality affordable rental homes; utilize housing as a platform for improving quality of life; build inclusive and sustainable communities free from discrimination, an transform the way HUD does business.

Homeless Children and Youth Act
(in the Every Student Succeeds Act of 2015),
aka McKinney-Vento Act (2-page summary as provided by SchoolHouse Connection)

SchoolHouse
Connection

MCKINNEY-VENTO ACT 2-PAGE SUMMARY: HOMELESS CHILDREN AND YOUTH IN THE EVERY STUDENT SUCCEEDS ACT OF 2015

This brief document summarizes ESSA's provisions on homelessness, with links to key implementation resources.

At the State Agency Level

Every State Education Agency (SEA) must designate an Office of State Coordinator that can sufficiently carry out duties in the Act.[i] Key duties include:

- Posting on the SEA website an annually updated list of local educational agency (LEA) liaisons, and the number of homeless children and youth LEAs identify statewide.[ii]
- Responding to inquiries from homeless parents and unaccompanied youth.[iii]
- Providing professional development programs for liaisons and others.[iv]
  (*Resource*: *McKinney-Vento PPT that can be edited and repurposed in states.*)
- Monitoring LEAs to enforce compliance.[v]

At the Local Agency Level

Every LEA must designate a liaison (*Resource: Guidelines for Designating Liaisons*) for students experiencing homelessness who is able to carry out the duties described in the law.[vi] Key duties include:

- Ensuring that homeless children and youth are identified and enrolled in school, and have a full and equal opportunity to succeed in school.[vii]
  (*Resource*: *A SHC webinar with McKinney-Vento liaisons and State Coordinators sharing strategies for identifying eligible students.*)
- Participating in professional development and other technical assistance offered by the State Coordinator.[viii]
- Ensuring that school personnel receive professional development and other support.[ix]
- Ensuring that unaccompanied homeless youth are informed, and receive verification, of their status as independent students for college financial aid.[x] (*Resource*: *Higher Education for Youth Experiencing Homelessness*)
- Ensuring that homeless children, youth, and families receive referrals to health, dental, mental health, housing, substance abuse, and other appropriate services.[xi]

- Disseminating public notice of McKinney-Vento rights in locations frequented by parents and youth, in a manner and form understandable to them.[xii]

School Stability

- Homeless children and youth can remain in their school of origin for the duration of homelessness and until the end of an academic year in which they obtain permanent housing.[xiii]
- LEAs must make best interest determinations about school selection that presume that staying in the school of origin is in the best interest of the child or youth; consider specific student-centered factors; prioritize the wishes of the parent, guardian, or unaccompanied youth; and include a written explanation and right to appeal if the LEA determines that school stability is not in the best interest of the child or youth.[xiv]
- The definition of school of origin now includes both the designated receiving school at the next grade level (if there is a feeder school pattern), and preschools.[xv] (*Resource*: *Preschool to Prevent Homelessness*)
- Transportation to the school of origin is required, including until the end of the academic year when a student obtains permanent housing (if it is in the student's best interest to remain in that school).[xvi]

School Enrollment and Full Participation

- Homeless children and youth must be enrolled in school immediately, even if they lack documents or have missed application or enrollment deadlines during any period of homelessness.[xvii]
- SEAs and LEAs must develop, review, and revise policies to remove barriers to the identification, enrollment, and retention of homeless students in school, including barriers due to fees, fines, and absences.[xviii]

Link to webpage with resources: https://www.schoolhouseconnection.org/mckinney-vento-act-two-page-summary/

- If a dispute arises over eligibility, school selection or enrollment, the child or youth must be immediately enrolled in the school in which the parent, guardian or unaccompanied youth seeks enrollment, pending resolution of the dispute, including all available appeals.[xix]
- States must have procedures to ensure that homeless children and youth do not face barriers to accessing academic and extracurricular activities.[xx] (*Resource: Full Participation in Extra-Curricular Activities*)

Preschool Children

- The definition of school of origin includes preschools.[xxi]
- Liaisons must ensure homeless families and children can access Head Start, Early Head Start, LEA-administered pre-school programs and early intervention services under IDEA Part C, if eligible. [xxii] (*Resource: Pathways to Partnership Early Childhood*)

Credit Accrual and College Readiness

- States must have procedures to identify and remove barriers that prevent students from receiving appropriate credit for full or partial coursework satisfactorily completed while attending a prior school, in accordance with State, local, and school policies.[xxiii] (*Archived Webinar: Getting to Graduation: Strategies to Award Partial Credits, Recover Credits, and Award High School Diplomas for Students Experiencing Homelessness*)
- State plans must describe how homeless youth will receive assistance from school counselors to advise, prepare, and improve their readiness for college.[xxiv] (*Resource: Quick Guide for Counseling Staff*)

Definition of Homelessness

- The McKinney-Vento definition of homelessness includes children and youth who lack a fixed, regular, and adequate nighttime residence.[xxv]
- This definition specifically includes children and youth who are: sharing the housing of others due to loss of housing, economic hardship, or a similar reason; living in shelters, transitional housing, or cars; and staying in motels or campgrounds due to lack of adequate alternative accommodations.[xxvi]
- The phrase "awaiting foster care placement" was deleted from the McKinney-Vento Act. New protections for all children in foster care were included under Title I Part A.[xxvii] (*Resource: Transportation for Students in Foster Care*)

Title I, Part A

- All LEAs that receive Title I Part A funds must reserve funds to support homeless students.[xxviii] (*Resource: Two-Page Summary of Title I and Homelessness*)
- Reserved funds may be used for services not ordinarily provided by Title I, including local liaisons and transportation to the school of origin.[xxix]
- State report cards must include disaggregated information on the graduation rates and academic achievement of homeless children and youth.[xxx] (*Education Leads Home Homeless Student State Snapshots share identification, graduation and achievement data*)

i 42 U.S.C. §11432(d)(3).
ii 42 U.S.C. §§ (g)(6)(B); (f)(1).
iii 42 U.S.C. §(f)(7).
iv 42 U.S.C. §(f)(6).
v 42 U.S.C. §(f)(5).
vi 42 U.S.C. §(g)(1)(J)(ii).
vii 42 U.S.C. §§ (g)(6)(A)(i)-(ii).
viii 42 U.S.C. §(g)(1)(J)(iv).
ix 42 U.S.C. §(g)(6)(A)(ix).
x 42 U.S.C. §(g)(6)(A)(x)(III).
xi 42 U.S.C. §(g)(6)(A)(iv).
xii 42 U.S.C. §(g)(6)(A)(vi).
xiii 42 U.S.C. §(g)(3)(A).
xiv 42 U.S.C. §(g)(3)(B).
xv 42 U.S.C. §(g)(3)(I).

xvi 42 U.S.C. §(g)(1)(J)(iii).
xvii 42 U.S.C. §(g)(3)(C).
xviii 42 U.S.C. §(g)(1)(I).
xix 42 U.S.C. §(g)(3)(E)(i).
xx 42 U.S.C. §(g)(1)(F)(iii).
xxi 42 U.S.C. §(g)(3)(I).
xxii 42 U.S.C. §(g)(6)(A)(iii).
xxiii 42 U.S.C. §(g)(1)(F)(ii).
xxiv 42 U.S.C. §(g)(1)(K).
xxv 42 U.S.C. §11434a(2).
xxvi 42 U.S.C. §11434a(2).
xxvii ESSA §§9105(b) and (c).
xxviii 20 U.S.C. §6313(c)(3)(A).
xxix 20 U.S.C. §6313(c)(3)(C)(ii).
xxx 20 U.S.C. §§6311(h)(1)(C)(ii) and (iii).

Link to webpage with resources: https://www.schoolhouseconnection.org/mckinney-vento-act-two-page-summary/

INDEX